From Buckets To Big Bucks

LaWanda Thomas

Copyright © 2018 Author Lawanda Thomas

Writer's University publishing house

All rights reserved.

DEDICATION

To my three daughters, ArDaysha, Mia and Skylar. All I've ever wanted was to show you all the best things in life. It was a rough fight in the beginning, but we survived with the help of God. Remember, anything you put your mind to, you're able to! You've watched me struggle so you wouldn't have to. I've paved the way so you can soar!

Love you all to Life

CONTENTS

	Acknowledgments	i
1	Fired Up and Out	3
2	Surviving Off of $238	13
3	Fish Out of Water	24
4	Maybe This Isn't For Me	34
5	When Tragedy Hits	44
6	Bossing Up	53
7	Started From the Bottom and Now I'm Here	65
8	Balance	72
9	Epilogue	82

ACKNOWLEDGMENTS

To my parents, Emma & Fredrick Dortch. Thank you for having my back financially, and working in the business with me. From driving, and doing everything you could to ensure I didn't fall with Regal Touch, I am so grateful.

Thank you to my daughters for sticking it out with me and letting me pursue my purpose. Bishop and Lady Vivian Jacobs, thank you for mentorship, and spiritual guidance in everything I do. Thank you for the genuine support!

Thank you to my friend, Latisha Morris for being a true friend from day 1. You have been there since the birth of Regal Touch. You even helped me name it. Now you're here for my first book, and you helped me name this. Thank you for all you've done!

Thank you to Keynote, for editing my book. Writers University, for publishing it. I would like to thank every client, and support of Regal Touch Maid Cleaning Service. Thank you to everyone who played a part in helping with ideas, being a listening ear or just being a blessing financially. I would like to say Thank you.

Lawanda Thomas
CEO and Founder of, Regal Touch Maid and Cleaning Service

1

FIRED UP AND OUT

My heart skipped a beat and my chest begin to tighten. I couldn't believe what I was reading. That text message must be wrong. I had to pick my phone up to get a closer look at it. The message read "Your services are no longer needed. In two weeks, come pick up your last check, and return any items that belong to us." I couldn't believe what I was reading. I was frozen and speechless. The cars behind me were blowing because the light had turned green. I quickly pulled over to the side of the road. I was in utter disbelief. I was only fifteen minutes away from work. I checked the clock to see if I was late. I tried to remember if I had been asked to come in early and had forgotten. I sat in my car on the side of the road in silence. *Is this really happening?* I couldn't believe that I had just been fired from my job that I had worked for almost six years.

My mind began to race. *What do I do next? Should I text back, call, or go up there? How, can you be so heartless and not tell me to my face?* Thoughts of rage and anger began to race through my mind. After a while, I called to get answers. The receptionist answered and said that my now former boss was unavailable to talk. I hung up and immediately called the cell phone number from which the text message had come. It went straight to voicemail. I sent a text message asking if I had done anything that prompted me being fired. Again, no response!

I continued sitting in my car wondering what I had done wrong. I need to go up there and make them look me in my face and fire me the right way. I have never been let go of a job before. I was just at work yesterday and no one said anything! In twenty-four hours, I have gone from employed to unemployed. After all the hard work and late hours I gave them. They have some nerve treating me this way! I was loyal to them. People would quit left and right and I stayed. I would work two and three positions at a time. I gave up my weekends to help and I did it, without pay! We were like family in there. I've been to their house for family functions. They have visited my church on "Family and Friends Day". I mean, when they went out of town, they entrusted me with keys and alarm codes to the business. I have used the company credit cards to handle business matters on their behalf. What happened? Did I miss a sign somewhere that said "Throw me away like trash when you're done using me up"? It's two weeks before Christmas. What do I tell my daughters? Honestly, in that moment I felt like I had been used.

As I turned my car around to drive back home, my mind began to take me back to review the last year. I started to think about how unhappy I had been feeling working there. Every day, I would sit at my desk and say, "This can't be my life. There's got to be more for me than this." There had been many days of feeling unappreciated and just tolerated at work because they had a high turnover rate and couldn't seem to keep employees. Now, here I am almost six years in and I have nothing to show for it. Living paycheck to paycheck, having to borrow money from people, taking out title loans and paycheck advances just to make it. As sad as it was, I had gotten comfortable in the state that I was in and even though I would complain, my situation had become the norm for me. I was working to get by with no hopes of seeing beyond my situation.

I continued to think about the many days that I had

struggled to get up and get dressed to go into work. I thought about how I been pushing someone else's dreams and helping to birth another person's vision. I was loyal to them because they were black business women and started from nothing. They had worked hard and had somehow managed to be in business for almost 20 years. In many ways, I admired them and wanted to be like them. I was grateful they had given me a job with no experience so at times I took unfair treatment when I didn't have to. In the beginning years of me being there, I was willing to learn every position in the company, in hopes that I would move up to a higher position and make a career out of it. I was okay with having no benefits or insurance because I thought I would eventually get a raise for all of my hard work. Sadly, I found out the hard way that even though I was willing to learn more they certainly weren't willing to pay more.

No matter how much I learned, I would never surpass them because it was their vision and my job was just to keep the business going to make them money. Year after year I would apply for jobs while still working there but no other job opportunity had presented itself. What was I to do? *Guess I'm stuck here,* I thought.

I learned that complaining and being bitter wasn't helping me leave that job any sooner. I had to learn to change my thinking and my behavior towards the situation. Once, I changed my mindset it became easier to go to work. This is why I was in a state of shock because I was actually coming to work happy and I was being productive while I was there. I gave 110% of my skills and abilities, working nine hours a day sometimes without a lunch break. I couldn't believe that God was allowing this to happen to me. I had finally found peace at this job and now this!

Let me stop it with the reminiscing and flashbacks. This is not helping me. I'm still fired! 'Snap out of it quick", is what I said to myself as I continued to drive, going nowhere. For some reason I found peace in seeing the sunshine peek out among the clouds in December. Just maybe this was God's way of speaking to me and letting me know that there is light ahead at the end of the tunnel. I kept driving until I found myself parking at a temp agency. I was determined to find a job before Christmas. I didn't want to ruin my daughters holiday.

As I sat in the temp agency filling out forms, I listened to people around me talk about how they had been there before. "These jobs don't make much". "It's hard to get a set schedule", they said. I instantly became discouraged. *This cannot be my life. There has to be more to life than this.*

A few minutes later, I was called in to meet with a job recruiter. He looked at my application for a few minutes and then looked up at me and asked, "Why are you here, again?" I began to explain to him that just a few hours prior to walking into his office I had been fired from my job. He began to read my qualifications and then he told me that I was overqualified for the jobs that they were offering. I looked at him and tears begin to roll down my face. He was the first person to hear about my story. I found myself crying in front of a complete stranger because the actual impact of my situation had finally hit me. I had no job, no savings, and no other source of income. My mind begin to race. *How will I pay my car note, rent, cell phone bill, and put food on the table for my girls and myself?*

As I wiped my face, the recruiter told me something that I would always remember. He said, "Anybody can work a job but very few people have the skills to create one." At that moment, I wondered what made him say that to me. In fact, I'm not sure he even realized that he said it. I was stung by the statement because it was so powerful but yet so true! This man had just blessed my life with those words and he did not even know me. I left out the office with still more questions. *God was that you speaking through this man? Is this your way of trying to get my attention? Should I be looking into creating my own business?* Still, no answer from God. It seemed that lately he was speaking through people more than speaking to me directly.

I drove home to an empty house because my girls were still in school. With no one around, I broke down and cried. I needed to release all that I was feeling because, somehow, I knew that where I was going I couldn't take the pain, hurt, and mixed emotions with me. I began to do what I knew best and that was to pray. I started praying for direction, peace, and wisdom. What was next for me? Truthfully, I really wasn't certain about what was next. The only thing I was sure of was that fact that I was tired of working for others. I was tired of barely making it and being stressed out from working only to find out that there is no reward in the end. I was tired of tossing and turning at night because I was too embarrassed to tell family and friends about what I was going through. The stress of not knowing what was next was eating me up inside.

On Wednesday night I went to Bible study like usual. It seemed as if my pastor was talking directly to me while he taught. I sat there in tears. He began to remind us that God had not forgotten about us and that although our situations may seem rough at the moment, God was still in control. That night I decided that it was time to pull my life together. No more crying and pity parties.

The wheels started turning in my head. *Why am I looking for a job? Do I really want to work for someone? Maybe I should find out what I'm good at? How can I make more than enough money to support myself and my family?* I began to google work from home businesses but it seemed like none of them were legit or piqued my interest. That's when I realized that I needed to get up and do something with myself. I refused to lay in defeat as if this was the end of my story. Yes, I had lost a job BUT at that job I had learned skills that could possibly help me create my own business.

I thought about a business plan that I had written some time before. The plan was for a cleaning service but I had never done anything with the plan because I didn't understand the full concept of writing it. So like so many other people who never put their ideas into action, the business was merely a dream. I hadn't put work into making the dream a reality. The notion of starting my own business and being my own boss had sounded fantastic. I could work when I felt like working, make my own hours, and no one could tell me what to do. It was great "idea" at the moment. It would be a goal I could work toward but because I needed a job at that moment it wasn't at the forefront of my mind. I pretty much threw the business plan aside and continued working my nine to five.

Given my present situation, I continued to apply online for jobs but no one was calling me in for interviews. I decided that since I was fired without cause, I would file for unemployment. To my surprise, filing for unemployment was a lot of work in itself. First, I had to apply online. Then I had to do a phone interview. The interview was set for a specific time that I could not miss because if I did, my claim could possibly be denied. After that, I had to meet with someone at the unemployment office and then wait for a letter in the mail to determine if I was approved. The letter took two weeks to come and it stated that my former employer had two weeks to respond to the claim.

Two more weeks went by. Still no job interviews had come through. I was just surviving off of my last paycheck that I had received. *Christmas is almost here. What do I tell my girls? How do I explain to them that I lost my job?* I was crushed knowing that I wouldn't be able to give them gifts for Christmas. I have always been a last minute shopper so it wasn't anything new for me to buy things days before Christmas. The issue was that I just couldn't afford to buy anything. I knew it would be hard to buy groceries just for Christmas Day alone, not to mention having enough food for the days after. I heard about food pantries at local churches that distributed food. I went. *I have nothing to lose. At least, we'll have Christmas dinner since I won't be able to provide any gifts this year.*

As Christmas was drawing near, the girls started asking questions. I knew then that I would have to tell them the truth soon. I had been borrowing money from my family to feed us and to put gas in my car to take them to school. I tried to keep things to myself but when they starting asking to get a Christmas tree and some decorations, I broke down and cried. My heart was heavy and I felt like I had let them down. Yes, I knew it wasn't my fault that I lost my job but it wasn't their fault either. Finally, I mustered up the strength to tell the girls what had happened. I could see in their eyes that they were more concerned about me than about Christmas. They had never seen me cry before or be sad in front of them like this. With tears rolling down my face, I began to tell them that I had lost my jobs two weeks prior. They stood there looking at me in silence. After a few minutes, they started with questions. "Will we have to move?" "Will we have to go live with our dad?" "What will happen to us, Mom?" At that moment, I had no answers for them. My baby girl kept asking questions. Still, I had no answers. My oldest daughter handed me some Kleenex and said, "God's got you Mom.

The bible says that He will never leave us or forsake us. We will be okay. Don't worry about Christmas. Christmas is about birth of Jesus, not us, anyway." I looked up at her in amazement. Who knew that my 14 year old daughter would be the encouragement that I needed to get up from where I was and see God in my situation!

A few days later, I received a text message inviting me to a networking event with some business owners and entrepreneurs. I remember looking at the text like, "why did she send this to me? That's not for me. I'll tell my friend who is an entrepreneur about it instead." Well, I sent my friend the text and of all people, she asked me to go with her to the event. Go figure.

The event was held downtown Chicago on an unusually cold night. As we got out of the car to go in the building, it began to snow. We didn't have umbrellas or hats on our head. We just ran into the building laughing and saying that "we should've stayed at home. This snow is too much but we're here now so we might as well go in."

Looking back, I can truly say that I am glad that we did go. The two hours we were there would change my life forever.

I remember walking into the room and seeing vendor tables set up all around. We were a little late so we found the closest seats by the door and began to listen to the speaker. The speaker was a dark skinned petite woman with a strong voice. She spoke with so much confidence and knowledge. She grabbed my attention instantly because she was sarcastic with a twist of arrogance, but in a good way. She was not rude or condescending. She was dressed for success but with a touch of sass. She began to run her resume off to us, making sure that we knew that she was more than capable to teach the workshop.

The event also had a panel comprised of women business owners and company CEOs. The information was limitless and they were so transparent with us. People were asking questions about how to start a business, what resources to use, and where to get money from to start a business. As people continued to ask questions, I just sat there and wondered, "Why am I even here?" My friend had a page of notes and the lady who invited us was asking plenty of questions. I continued to listen and take in what applied to me. One lady talked about the hardship of owning her business and how she almost gave up several times. Another lady talked about how her passion fueled her business.

I kept listening but nothing had really piqued my interest until we were asked to write three dates down on a piece of paper. These dates were to keep us on track concerning our business goals. Next to each date, we had to write down what we wanted to accomplish for our business. The speaker begin to say that if we didn't t have a business idea just yet, we could write down short terms goals for our lives. I wrote down the only thing I could think of, "I need a job to support my family". As I read what I had written, my eyes began to open and my ears became more Intune to what they were saying. It was almost at that moment that I found my purpose.

Once the event was over, people began to network and pass their business cards out. The guest speakers began to answer any personal questions that we had. I remember going up to one of the speakers. I liked her because of her demeanor and presentation. I felt that I was able to relate to her story. I remember her telling us that there was free funding available for women in business. When I approached her she was so down to earth and she was willing to answer all of my questions. I decided to mingle with other women there and began collecting business cards and literature from the different vendor tables.

I mingled throughout the conference area for quite some time before a young lady who had been a guest on one of my favorite reality shows walked up to me and asked me what I did for a living. With nothing to say, I flipped the conversation back to her and the reality show that she had been on. I had on this money green pea coat and she looked at me and said, " You look so Regal. You look like you own several businesses. You look like money!" I responded "Thank you" but in my mind I was thinking, "What does she mean by *'I look regal?'*" Another lady overheard our conversation and said, "You do look really regal." I was taken aback with their comments and their words really stuck with me.

As my friend and I walked to the car after the event, we started to talk about how inspired we were. I began to share my excitement and expressed to her that I had decided that I really did want to start a business after all. I finally knew what I wanted to do! I told her that I wanted to own a cleaning service that catered to homes and businesses. My friend looked at me and said, "A cleaning service, huh." I could sense in her voice that she thought I had lost my mind. As we were driving, she said, "Well if that's what you want to do then go ahead." I began googling cleaning services on the web while she drove. All of a sudden she asked me, "What will you name it?"

I began to tell her about my conversations at the

event. I told her about a few ladies saying that I looked regal. I looked up the word regal and it saw that it meant royal, relating to a king, queen, magnificent, or dignified. We continued to drive home pitching around names for the business. We had names like *Crisp Finish, Crisp Touch, Polish Finishing Cleaning service, and Elegant Finish* but none of them stuck out like *Regal*. I began to google businesses with the word "regal" in it and got instantly discouraged because I found several businesses with similar names. I didn't give up on the idea of owning the cleaning service but I just knew that it would take a little longer to find the name.

    Once I arrived home, I stayed up all night researching cleaning services and finding information on how to own one.

    The next morning, I woke up and checked the mail to see if my unemployment letter had arrived. Still nothing. I decided to apply online for some welfare assistance. I applied online, and to my surprise, I had to wait for another letter in the mail giving me a phone interview. I found myself getting angry and frustrated being told that I had to wait so long for help that I needed desperately. Days later, my unemployment letter finally came but I was only approved for six months and the amount I was to receive was $238.00 a week. Devastation hit me again. How w*as I supposed to live off this? What am I to do?*

    Later that day, my friend text me and began to talk about the entrepreneur event we had attended the night before. I went back to the few notes that I had taken. I started to google names for my cleaning services again. I finally came up with name *Regal Touch* and added *Maid and Cleaning Services* to it to make it my own. Tears of joy rolled down my face because just like that I had become a business owner!

2

SURVIVING OFF OF $238

It's official. Regal Touch Maid & Cleaning Services is more than an idea. It's now a business. I had such a feeling of accomplishment after I registered my business name with the state. Reality set in. It was time for me to see this thing through. I remember getting in my car after the clerk gave me a signed copy of my business name. I just sat there for a few minutes and looked at the paper in amazement. I couldn't believe that in matter of minutes my business had become recognized by the state. At that moment, I knew within myself that this was only the beginning of my story.

Yes, having a business plan would of been the realistic way of starting a business but nothing about my situation had been textbook thus far. I felt like I was pushed into my business by God because I certainly had no intention of jumping into it on my own. It's funny how we say we want something so bad but when opportunity presents itself we say, "It's too much, I'm not ready, or I need to wait until my money is right." I discovered that we only find ourselves getting more content in the state that we are in. I would rather say, "I tried it" than to say, "I want to" and never try!

Honestly, I would not have quit my job to start a business

with no direction and no money. I would have called someone crazy for leaving a paying job only to jump into the sea of uncertainty! Who in their right mind would take such a risk? I didn't know much about entrepreneurship but from what I had recently learned, entrepreneurs were risk takers. So since, I had jumped into the sea of uncertainty and started a business, I felt that it was better to row with the tide of the wave than row against it!

I found myself up countless nights researching ways to start a cleaning business. To my surprise, the internet was full of free and credible information. Who would of known it was this easy? I found step by step directions on what you needed to do and who you needed to talk to. There were also videos posted that showed how to clean residential and commercial properties. It was so much information that my eyes where burning at night from reading the small print on my laptop. It became overwhelming for a moment because I was on my own trying to figure out what would be best for my business. Some nights I didn't know how to take it all in. During the day I would be so beat and tired. I would only get up to drop my girls off at school, go back home to take a nap, and then continue searching for more information.

Before I knew it, I had stopped applying for jobs. I put all of my faith into knowing that I was going to make money with Regal Touch. I started getting so obsessed with building Regal Touch that my prayer life and bible study was suffering. I didn't realize it until one day when I fell asleep typing and started dreaming. In the dream, I saw myself reaching for something but I was having a hard time getting my hands on it. I could feel the strain from trying to grab whatever it was but the more I thought I was getting closer to grabbing it, the further away I found myself. It was dark and cold and I remember feeling like I needed to find a light. I kept telling myself that if I could find the light, I could grab whatever "it" was, and get out of there!

All of sudden, I woke up and heard a voice clearly say, "I am the light and as long as you stay with me, you will always be able to see." I knew then that the dream was God's way of getting my attention early and reminding me that He had brought me to that point and would continue to lead me.

I kept researching and learned that there were some important forms that I needed to fill out and pay for that would certify my business as a legal entity. I remember saying to myself, "I would rather start out the right way than to take shortcuts and kill my business before it really got started." The crazy part is that I wrote all of the information down then I called and got pricing and started paperwork online as if I had the money. There were fees for business licensing, business insurance, bonding insurance, and registering for sales tax licensing. There was paperwork on the legal structure of my business stating whether I wanted to be a sole proprietorship or a limited liability company. Additionally, there were recurring startup costs like renting business space, working capital, telephone, advertising, and supplies!

I knew I wasn't ready for a business office yet but I read that it was important for me to know about these expenses and how to use them when I filed my business taxes. So many expenses and no money.

All of my excitement began to leave my body because the numbers were getting bigger than my pockets. *Lord, what am I going to do? I barely have money to eat and pay bills. Maybe I should just skip the legal paperwork and just start cleaning properties. Once I make money I'll go back and take care of it!* Sounded good at the moment, until I started reading about how people could sue me and how people have the right to ask to see my insurance and license before cleaning their home or business. I knew then that I didn't want to have to deal with any of those issues so I needed a new plan to come up with the money that I needed.

During this time of the year, people were filing their income taxes and getting returns so I figured that this was the best time to borrow money from someone. Well actually, my first plan was to go to a payday loan place and borrow against the last check that I had received from work. "I'll just pay them back whenever I can", I thought. I went into the payday loan store. I had used their services before and I was in good standing with them so I figured that I would take my check stub and bank card in there like usual and get a loan. The cashier took all of my information and asked for my job telephone number and a contact person so that she could verify my employment. I instantly got sick to my stomach because I knew then that I was busted! I told the cashier that I had changed my mind and that she could just give me my information back. She asked me if there was a problem. Once again, I told her that I had just changed my mind. She returned my ID, bank card, and check stub. I left out of there feeling defeated.

Someone suggested that I try my bank but honestly, I knew that wasn't going to go well. I stayed in the red with them the majority of the time. Not to mention, I had just over drafted the max off my card days ago. Desperate times had called for desperate measures! It was time to put my pride aside and ask for help financially. I was already tired of getting help from my family and I was too ashamed to borrow from friends. *Should I give up now or continue?*

On the internet, I came across micro lenders that catered to women business owners and lower income minorities. These lenders would provide funds for expansion and money to buy equipment and inventory. I also found information about small business administration programs that were available to help with obtaining growth capital and connecting business owners to various other resource centers that offer assistance.

The only issue was that one of the program requirements was that the business had to have been in operation for a specified amount of years and had built credibility. Well, I had just started. Where was the money for people like me? Where's the help for those who don't have money sitting around? Those who don't have a inheritance? Those with credit that won't allow them to walk in a bank and get a loan? Those programs sounded good for those who fit the criteria but not for people like me.

I went on another website that allowed you to work with loan consultants. The consultants would assist you with business records, cash flow credit, credit issues, refer you to small business development centers, law firms, and banks. Of course no one had an answer on how to help a start-up business develop cash flow. I was becoming angry inside because it seemed as if the odds were stacked against me and there was no hope. How was I to pay for all of my legal paperwork so that I could start working? I had learned that there were 9 million women owned businesses in the USA that generate almost a trillion and a half in revenue and you mean to tell me no one thought of doing a funding program for first year business owners? I remember saying to myself, "What about us little people? What do we do?

It seems as if no one cares about us." But truth be told, everyone started like us! SBA (small business administration) reports that small businesses pay about 44.3% of the total private payroll in the United States and employ half of all private sector employees. It was small businesses that helped lead the country out of economic downturns in the 1980s and 1990s.

I knew that small businesses were needed. They were the backbone that often held the big companies up. I just was confused as to why there was no help for startup businesses. I soon began to see that being an entrepreneur would mean using my own personal money to survive until someone gave me a loan.

I still was dreading to ask my family for help. By chance, or maybe not, I ran into someone who worked for an investor. They were looking for small businesses to fund. Of course I was very skeptical to say the least, but honestly, I was desperate. I knew God had placed Regal Touch in my hands and it was up to me to make things happen. So, I couldn't let it go. I had to keep trying! Faith without works is dead, right?

I felt that the gentleman that referred me to this investor was very credible. I thought that because we were of the same faith, he would look out for me. So he began to tell me about all of the qualifications that were needed and the things that the investor would want to see. One thing needed was a bank statement that was issued in the business name. He would need to see the activity of money being deposited daily to get an idea of what I was bringing in on a monthly basis. Instantly, I became silent as a lamb on the phone with him. Inside, I was yelling, "Duh sir, my business just started. I really don't have any money coming in. This is the main reason I am looking for investors." Then he asked me about assets. Did I have anything that I could use to hold the loan with? More questions followed. What's your credit score? Do you have a cosigner? I replied "no" to all of his questions. Then he said, "I know you did a business plan before you started.

Let him see that so he knows the direction you're going in." Again, I replied, "No. I didn't do one." He began asking me why didn't I have one because most businesses start with one. I didn't have the answers he wanted to hear and the more he kept talking about it, the more I realized why I didn't write one and finish it in the beginning. I wanted to shout to the top of my lungs, "Is anyone listening to me? I need money! If I had it, I wouldn't be asking!!!"

We ended the conversation and I hung up the phone while frustrated tears rolled down my face. I could feel the hot drops coming out of my eyes and I could smell the saltiness of my tears. I sat down on my bed and begin weeping. *Lord, what am I to do? No one wants to help me.* I felt my prayer shifting to anger. *God why are you putting me through this? I didn't ask to lose my job. You allowed that to happen to me. I've been trying my best to exercise my faith and put action behind it. It seems that every step forward I take in the right direction is actually the wrong direction in your eyes and you send me back!* I laid in my bed of tears. At this point, I just didn't know how I would make it.

As I laid there, I picked up my cell phone and came across an article on the internet that talked about the qualities of a good entrepreneur. The article talked about how entrepreneurs come in all genders, age groups, and educational backgrounds. It talked about having passion, persistence, independence, self-reliance, and self-confidence. "Passion is the cornerstone of the entrepreneurial spirit." Once I saw that quote I began to question my passion for Regal Touch. *How confident am I about my ability to clean properties?* I started to understand that if I didn't believe in what I was selling then I couldn't expect anyone else to buy it. *Am I persistent? Will I stop and cry every time something doesn't go my way? Am I independent enough to make things happen with or without a loan or an investor?* As I continued reading the article I started to realize that I was my own hindrance in so many ways.

The next day, I forced myself to get up out of the bed. I had a pep talk with myself, reminding myself that a man and/or woman who doesn't work, doesn't eat. Besides, I had my kids to think about. I was feeling bad because they would ask for lunch money and I didn't have money to give them. I needed every penny that came in the household to help us survive until the next month. The girls were asking to go places with their friends and they would say, "Don't worry about the money. My friend's mom will pay." Did they know how that made me feel? As a mother, it felt like my girls were becoming charity cases to people.

I knew that it wasn't right for me to make them stay in the house because I was broke but my momma had always taught me that as a parent, you never let your child go anywhere without money. It was becoming one embarrassing moment after another.

I'll never forget the day that I went to a women's fellowship around this time. I really didn't want to go because it was at a fancy restaurant and I barely had gas to get there, let alone eat. I went anyway. By now, a few of the women in my church knew about my situation. I remember sitting at the table with everyone and when the waiter gave me the menu, I wanted to cry. I had no money. *Why did I even come?* I was not accustomed to not have any money at all. nothing to at least buy something to eat. Yes, I struggled and was in debt a lot with my job but I had comfort in knowing that with a job I at least knew I had steady income. Now, I had virtually nothing. Being oblivious to the full plight of my financial situation, everyone started ordering their meals. The waiter asked me for my order. "I'll pass for tonight", I said, while handing him the menu.

    I felt like all eyes were on me. One lady after the next started asking questions. Is everything ok? Are you sure that you're not hungry? Are you fasting? Did you eat before you got here? I know they meant no harm but I was embarrassed and devastated. I gathered enough strength and said, "I'm fine, thank you." They had no idea that I only came because I felt obligated. Our fellowship that night was a time to celebrate our "secret Santa" holiday gift exchange. I had had a job when we pulled names weeks ago and I didn't want to not show up to give my secret sister her gift. I excused myself from the table and went to the bathroom. Inside the stall, I cried. I felt so horrible and hopeless. I couldn't even afford a salad!

    I composed myself as best as I could and prepared to walk back to the table. As I began walking back into the room, I felt as if everyone was watching me, as if they felt sorry for me. We laughed and talked some more and then the food arrived at the table. I decided to get up again and go into the lobby as if I was taking a phone call while they ate. I just couldn't take everyone asking me if I was alright. I came back in for a brief moment and took the opportunity to give my secret sister her gift and then left.

    Snow fell heavily as I drove home. I looked down at my gas gage and sighed. I had just enough gas in my car to get home. The further I drove the more upset I became with myself. I realized that I was beginning to play the victim. It was time to go to work on this business idea. This was the moment that I had to trust God solely! I had to trust and believe that He hadn't brought me this far to leave me. I couldn't have a pity party or go into isolation. I needed to change my perception about my situation but first I needed to go back to God the right way and ask him to forgive me and my selfish ways. I had been so focused on making Regal Touch the answer to my situation that I had started putting my faith in it, instead of God. I began to pray and ask God for direction, grace, and favor as I started on this path.

After I prayed, I continued to research business ideas and resources. I still needed the finances to at least get started with the business. I decided that I would look beyond myself and pride and ask for help. I needed help! I went to my mom and told her about my business idea. I told her about the start-up costs and fees and that I needed to pay those things to get started. To my surprise, she asked, 'how much does it cost?" I began to run the numbers down to her. She got up, walked away, and came back a few minutes later. She handed me her debit card. Again, I was surprised. I asked her if she needed to see a breakdown of the fees or the receipt. She looked at me and replied, "No, just do what you said that you were going to do!"

I sat there humbled and in awe. What and who I needed was in front of me the entire time. I was too blind to see because I assumed that she wouldn't help me.

From a young age, I could recall my mom saying, "If you want something you've got to go out and get it. Nobody will just hand you anything and if they do, make sure to ask questions before taking it." I had been working since I was fourteen years old. All I knew was how to get out and work for I wanted. If you did things for yourself, no one could take credit for your accomplishments. I had watched my mom work two and three jobs never being home because she had to keep food on the table. She often took the bus and train to work, coming in late, and leaving early. I often wondered if she ever slept! I grew up watching this most of my life. She was the breadwinner in my home. I never knew until I got much older, that I had adapted her attitude and work ethics.

I found it hard for me to accept help or to ask for it. It took quite a while for me to realize that there are some genuine people out here who want to see others prosper with no intent to gain anything for themselves. Years of thinking "get it yourself" had been embedded in me. It was hard to accept things from people without thinking that they would tell people how they had helped me. You know, just to make themselves look good. I honestly felt that my mom meant well but that do it yourself mindset was how she had survived so she taught me all that she knew. I wasn't born with a silver spoon in my mouth, that is why I had to stop all of this crying and feeling sorry for myself. My job was gone but I was still alive, with breath in my body, and the activity of my limbs. I was going to make it!

I submitted the necessary legal paperwork to get my business going. I also continued to apply for jobs online. In the midst of everything, my family still had food, I had gas in my car, and we still had a roof over our head. My faith continued to increase and God began to show up on my behalf in unusual ways. As things began to get in place, it became easier to trust God, simply because I had everything that I needed in Him! I began to feel better. In fact, I felt even better on the day that I received an email confirming that my business had been approved by the state. Now, it was really time to prepare for the Regal Touch grand opening !

Things were looking up but still no jobs interviews came. One particular day, I decided to go to the mailbox instead of sending my daughter. All of it looked like the usual junk mail and bills. I kept shifting through mail and noticed that there was an envelope from the unemployment office. I opened it immediately and began reading the letter. I instantly got excited to see that I had been approved for six months of unemployment. Yes, to many $238.00 would have been discouraging, but I rejoiced. I was grateful. For me, it was a sign that God was yet working on my behalf.

I decided to make a budget. I was determined to pay my rent and my utilities. Once I got Regal Touch rolling, I was sure that I would be able to pay my other bills as well. I began to see beyond my circumstances and started seeing into my future. Things were looking up and now I needed to build a clientele. Once again, I needed help.

I reached out to two of my friends that were aspiring entrepreneurs as well. I asked them to meet me at a local coffee shop. I told them that I needed to shoot my ideas around to them and get their take on what I should do next. I knew both of them were very savvy with social media, so I openly admitted that I didn't know what I was doing with this whole business idea and that I definitely didn't know what I was doing when it came to social media. They knew about Regal Touch but I had been doing a lot of the research on my own. If I didn't think I needed help before I certainly realized it while I set there with them.

3

FISH OUT OF WATER

I was a fish out of water! I didn't know about anything that they were talking about. I remember sitting in the coffee shop with my friends as I listened to them go back and forth about social media. They were talking about who they were following and who had the most followers. I honestly felt old, outdated, and slightly dumb for a second. I continued to listen to them and the more I listened, I began to realize that I needed people around me who knew what I didn't know. We all need those type of people around us in business situations and life in general. Far too often, we become intimidated when we find ourselves in the company of others that know what we don't know.

We underestimate ourselves and miss out on networking and vital information. It's ok not to know, that's how you grow. If you're the smartest person in your circle, it's time for more friends.

I've learned that it is beneficial to surround yourself with people who have been where you are trying to go or have the knowledge to help get you there. I continued to sit there like a sponge soaking in everything that I heard. We began discussing our businesses ideas, goals, and future dates. We all agreed that a huge part of business success seemed to be because of social media. Businesses seemed to put a lot of effort in to having strong marketing on social media sites. I honestly didn't know how a cleaning service would benefit from social media. Truthfully, I had rarely, if ever, seen ads or posts about cleaning services. My plan was to just take some flyers and go from business to business hoping someone would give my cleaning service a chance. I asked my friends about ways that I could use social media to my advantage regarding my business. We kept talking and finally, I said, "If it is left up to me, I'll put some ads in the local newspaper". My friends quickly shot that idea down. Thankfully, they had some great ideas that trumped my newspaper ad approach. Hey, that's what friends are for, right?

Meeting with my friends really broadened my business perspective regarding marketing. More ideas about marketing and branding started coming up. I learned that a huge part of the marketing is about making the business appealing, like eye candy. People pay more attention to colors, prints, and words. I had so many thoughts and questions running through my head. *What could I do to make Regal Touch stand out? What colors will pop? What graphic designs are good strategies for cleaning services?* I had so many questions that I needed answered and so many things that I needed to do, including making business cards, flyers, logo, and a website. To my surprise, there were free apps on the internet that would help with some of my "to-do list items" until I could afford to pay someone for their services.

So, I figured that instead of complaining about the money that I didn't have, I would use the free resources that I had found. There was so much stuff to do and truthfully, I wasn't ready. I sat there and continued to listen and take notes. One thing on this journey that I had quickly learned was to not let fear cripple me from trying. I got super excited just knowing that my business was actually happening.

As much as I was excited, I also had a few reservations. I wasn't accustomed to asking people for money, setting prices, or having to sell a service in order to provide for my family. The success of Regal Touch would be contingent on how many people I would talk to, advertising, and marketing. I believed wholeheartedly in my business endeavor and I was going to make it work! I'm an "all-in" in type of person and I thrive when I see the results of effort and work. With that being said, I vowed to make Regal Touch operate in excellence. I continued to do more research to find ideas to make Regal Touch more marketable

Part of my research included looking at established cleaning companies. When starting a business, understanding your market and potential competitors. You need to know what competitors offer and how they market things, so I did cold calling to get prices for cleaning services. I filled out questionnaires to get price quotes, signed up for emails, called companies, I did it all. I learned that it was difficult to actually speak to a person on the telephone and I learned that the internet questionnaires were usually long, boring, and asked questions that I didn't know the answers to. I also disliked that the interactions that I did have with some of the customer service representatives. Many of them were informal, unengaging, or impersonal. I wanted to have a different approach for Regal Touch.

Sure, I would be providing a service, but I also I wanted to create a memorable experience for customers. I wanted to meet the customer and have them express their wants, needs, and expectations. Clients spend money to have services that they prefer and I wanted to provide quality service. I decided to take the negative energy and bad experience to create a strategy to market my business and place Regal Touch in a class of its own. I knew that to be successful I would have to step out of my comfort zone, be more open, friendly, and approachable.

Being approachable and friendly were two business goals that I had set. Those goals seem to be straightforward and rather easy but personally those were very touchy subjects for me. In fact, I did not consider myself to be strong in those areas. I saw them as a shortcoming in my personality. I had never really thought of how my childhood actions were creeping up into my adulthood or would affect me until that very moment.

I can recall being a kid and growing up as an only child for a while. I was always alone, without friends. Most people would of thought I was spoiled but I wasn't. Yes, my mom made sure that I had what I needed but spoiled, nope, that definitely was not the case. I was quiet and at times , I was distant from the world. I would stay in my room a lot. My mom always had some type of animal at home for me to care of, play with, and talk to. So when I wasn't talking to Tony the cat, I was talking to my stuffed animals. I mean I didn't have a cell phone or Internet like kids have today to keep me company. Not only that, but friends where few because my momma's favorite line was "you don't need friends, I'm your friend". When she would say things like that I would sit in my room angry and crying. I always felt like she just wanted me to be lonely.

It was difficult to relate to other people. In fact, I found it extremely challenging to start conversations with others. Only at church did I actually socialize and it was hard there, too. I also dealt with bullying at school. I was teased and talked about because of my dark skin. I really disliked seeing the school kids because they were by far the most cruel towards me. I found myself not smiling and walking around frowning at everybody. Years of feeling unwanted, years of feeling ugly on the inside and outside started to take a toll on me. I starting building up a wall. I held things inside because I didn't know who I could trust. Insecurity overwhelmed me and isolated all the more. So for years, I just kept diaries of the pain that I felt. Looking back, I know that it was only by the grace of God that I had not committed suicide. Even in my youth, my relationship with God had given me strength.

As I matured, the way that I perceived myself changed as well. When I became a mother, my views changed even more. I had daughters and I vowed to not let my low self-esteem adversely affect them. I vowed to believe in myself and to accept the beauty that started back at me each time I looked in the mirror.

Now listen, I know you may be wondering why I mentioned my issues with abandonment, low self-esteem, and childhood bullying. Well, in starting my business I learned that unresolved issues and bad experiences can affect your future provision if you choose not to confront the issues, learn from them, and change. I carried those issues for years. As I stated before, those issues affected my friendships or lack of them but they also affected my work relationships as well. I would work jobs with people and wouldn't say much other than, "hello", or show myself to be friendly. Regal Touch was my future and it was service based business, so I definitely needed to work out my issues. I purposed to give excellent customer service to every customer whether online or in person that I would connect with.

So often, we pray for God to take us to our wealthy place, but if we're not healed from past hurt before entering into that new place, we may be walking into a wilderness instead. I know that if God had not healed me it would be impossible today to interact with anyone. In fact, I would venture to say that my business probably would not have happened without God healing me on the inside. God had to heal me, so that I would know how to treat others, how to approach customers with confidence, and how to have healthy conversations.

I continued to research more things to help my business. I wanted to know the good and the bad of the business world so I began researching main issues that negatively impact small businesses. Lack of planning, poor credit, lack of support, poor management skills, lack of money, bad customer experience, lack of resources, lack of experience, and poor cash management seemed to be the main issues. Instead of finding solutions, I wanted to prevent those things from even being present in my business. Admittedly, some things like lack of money and bad credit may take a while to conquer but I was refusing to let it stop me completely.

On the contrary, the positive things that impact small businesses owners include: focus, confidence, creativity, delegating responsibility, determination, independence, resources, marketing, and taking risks, just to name a few. I found peace in seeing that a lot of what was listed was already a part of my personality. However, the one trait that troubled me the most was creativity. Admittedly, I am not the most creative thinker at times, so I began to ask God to give me ideas or money to pay someone to work creatively on my behalf. I also knew that delegating tasks and responsibilities would be difficult for me because I tend to do things myself knowing that things will be done to my expectations. However, my research had helped me understand the importance of discovering my weaknesses and coming up with solutions to get things done in spite of them.

One way to accomplish that would be to hire someone to do projects for me and also train people to do things to help further my business. At some point I would need employees to help me complete the work and to also help run certain aspects of the business. After reading these things, I began to ask myself a series of questions. *Am I ready to be an entrepreneur? What do I want from my business? Is this just money to make it? Is it for financial inde*pendence, *or is for the satisfaction* of *knowing that I built and created income for my family and others?* Those were just a few of the questions that I asked myself.

Well, I have always had a heart to give, so I know that through my business I would be able to give a service to my clients, a source of income for employees, and provision for my family. The more I thought, I realized that providing for my family was of the utmost importance but even more than that I wanted to leave behind something for my kids to be proud of. Now days you don't see a lot of people leaving legacies behind for the generations to come. Well, I decided that I would start in my family and that Regal Touch would be the beginning of the legacy.

I just needed to stay focus and remember why I started the business in the first place. Remembering your "why" will help you continue searching for the "what's next" for your business!

From the conversation with my friends, I learned a lot, especially about marketing. However, from doing research I learned just how crucial marketing can be. It truly can either make or break your business! There are so many different ways to market that you must assess what works for your business.

Age, gender and race can play a huge part in your marketing. Yes, I know they tell us not to discriminate in business and you want to appeal to every buyer, but truthfully, every buyer will not be for you and you have to be okay with knowing that. Knowing who to target and how to grab their attention so they can buy your product or service is what matters most. I began to learn early in my business to focus and prefect what I have before going after more and never mastering anything. Listed In the chart below are some questions to think about pertaining to marketing when you are starting out.

How will I reach potential customers?	What is my target market?	What will set my business apart from my competitors?
How will customers find out about my business?		How much should I be spending on marketing?

    If you are providing a service, you will at some time have to think about pricing, unless you are starting a non-profit. Pricing was a nightmare in the beginning of business for me. Mainly because I didn't know the worth of what I offered. I searched online for information about the difference between hourly and flat fees. I learned that hourly rates had benefits because you could charge more and if you worked fast it would benefit the business with less work time spent and more pay. The downfall was that by being a new company, time was not always on my side. I was still learning what techniques worked for me and some things took more time to do than I had allotted for. So ,for an example, if a customer wants a service to be completed in four hours but it takes me longer to complete the service, the customer would rightfully be upset.
    True, I could say that the work that was completed in that time span was what they paid for but I didn't want to start

a business by giving poor service. Flat rate can have more negative points than positive because whatever you charge, that's it and however long it takes will determine your profit or lack thereof. Starting out my thoughts were to charge flat rates because I could be clear on how long a service would take and I wanted to make sure that I completed the job thoroughly.

Well, in the beginning it was a horror show for me. Yes, the work was getting done but I was moving too slow. Basically only one job was getting completed a day. The price I was charging was already slightly lower than other companies because I wanted to get their business by being cheaper. However, another factor was that I didn't know the value in myself as a business and the services that I provided. So because I didn't know how much I was worth, no one else did neither. In terms of a consumer, they are concerned with getting a good price and that the job is done. As a business owner, I was the one who had to change my mindset in order to get paid in accordance to what I was worth.

Isn't it ironic how things in our life have a lasting impact? Not knowing my worth or my value as a person was affecting how I presented my business and sold my service to others. That viewpoint was something that had affected me in my youth and now it was an issue in my business endeavor. I had never seen myself as someone that people took serious or would listen to. I sold myself cheap to get attention only to find out that I was hurting myself, not them. I was willing to work my tail off for cheap to get the business but I learned early that cheap prices don't necessarily keep business. I had to train myself to work faster, yet still use thorough techniques to clean.

So yep, you guessed it, I did some more research! I began watching videos on how to clean difficult areas and I went to stores to learn what products worked the best. Yes, I needed to set comparable prices and stop selling myself short but I also needed to provide the kind of work that is worth paying for.

The blessing was that while I was learning how to

market my business, God was setting up people to sow into it. I would of never reaped my harvest if I had got discouraged and stopped. It's amazing how God sets things up for us but He waits to release it until He see how serious we are.

    I had provided free service for a customer as a way to market myself in hopes to keep the client and possibly gain more. Well, the customer was pleased with my cleaning, so much that he began giving me referrals, started marketing me on his social media page, AND most of all, he continued his service with me! I was blessed by all of his support so I wasn't looking for anything else from him. Well, one morning after I finished cleaning his house, he started asking me about the marketing tools that I used to promote my business. I explained what I was doing and the plans I had for the future. We talked more and he shared tips to help me. I was grateful because people don't have to share what they know with you and they are not obligated to help you grow.

    I got in my car and shortly I received a text from the customer that I had just left. In the text, he said that he wanted to pay for a photo shoot for me so that I could have professional pictures for my business. I almost tore the bottom of my car up on Chicago potholes because I was so overwhelmed with joy. I hadn't even thought about a photo shoot! I was already on cloud nine because I had just recently met someone and they had decided to sow into me by gifting some business cards because they heard about what I was trying to do and wanted to help. That person bought 1000 business cards to start me out. Now, I was being gifted a photo shoot and all I had to do was show up. My makeup would be done for me as well. Tears began to flow down my face. I had to pull over and tell God thank you because that was what I needed at that moment to push me a little further.

    I had been excited to start my business. I was so grateful for my first customer, and although I knew her, I was happy that she was giving me an opportunity as a new business. I just knew I was on the roll but time had passed and no one was calling for Regal Touch. I had been putting flyers out, going

to businesses to introduce myself, and I had been giving out my business cards everywhere! No one was calling. So when I got to this particular customer
and he saw that my business was good soil to sow seeds in, I knew this was all God's handiwork saying, "Push harder this the beginning."

After that day, my faith increased a little more. I began to feel appreciated for my work. I began to remind myself, "You've got this." I began to push pass what I couldn't see at the time. Honestly, when no one is calling your business or giving you a chance, you're living off of $238.00 a week for income, and you have bills to pay and mouths to feed, it doesn't take much to discourage you. I was out there trying to make my vision a reality but until that point, it wasn't doing anything but bleeding the leftovers in my pockets and causing me to stay up at night wondering how to get gas money to face another day.

Getting those business cards and a photo shoot without me asking or doing anything for them, showed me that God can use anybody to bless you. He's just waiting on you to get in the right position to receive it. Be encouraged and know that your faith can increase! Sometimes, it just takes an act of kindness to give your faith an extra boost.

4

MAYBE THIS ISN'T FOR ME

The beginning of the year was all about getting marketing together and building clientele. Both were challenging. Eventually, a lady I knew gave me an opportunity to clean her apartment once a week. I was overjoyed because at least I had a chance to work and make some money. At some point, she referred my company to her sorority sisters and days later I was doing a walk through for a nail salon. I remember going to meet the owner and she expressed to me how happy she was that I was black owned business. She began to ask me questions, including how long I had been in business, if I was insured, and how many employees I had. I didn't want to start off lying to seem like I was more than what I was so I replied, "Regal Touch just got started weeks ago and right now all I have is myself and my brother if I need help."

She still was willing to give me a chance and I made sure that I exceeded her expectations every two weeks when I went. That conversation reaffirmed to me the importance of providing great service based solely on the expectation of the client. People have preferences and that is fine. No matter what, be sure to provide service that you take pride in and service that meets the expectations of the customer.

I kept hitting the streets in the cold and the wind trying to increase my clientele. In fact, I picked at least one day a week and hit the streets in busy areas that had beauty shops, barber shops, daycares, and nail salons. Some of the shops would let me in and others wouldn't. When I did get in, I would introduce myself, tell them the services that I offered, and leave my business cards. There were moments when I was walking in the cold, that all kinds of thoughts would cloud my mind. *I'm in way over my head. No one in these shops are going to give me a chance. They probably won't call.* Well, I'm glad I didn't give up because the last shop on this one particular block called. The owner had a popular beauty salon and she called me for my services. I was so excited! I remember hanging up the phone crying because I was starting to see my situation turn around for the good.

    I ended my first full month of business with three clients. I know that may not have been a lot and for some that number would have caused them to give up and get a job, but I was encouraged. I couldn't give up because I could see my business growing. Before I had even started my business I had written a list of places I wanted to service. Nail salons and beauty shops were on that list, so that's why I couldn't quit. My list was coming to life one customer at a time. I was determined to make my business a success.

    By this time, tax season was here, and honestly, I was happy. There were so many things I needed for my home and for my business. Listen, I had plans for my money, honey! I had been struggling financially and that money would definitely be a help. That's why I was in shock, disbelief, and panic when I had difficulty filing my taxes. For the first time in eighteen years of filing taxes, I had issues. Go figure. I filed my taxes in hopes of getting a return back in four weeks. Unfortunately, that four weeks turned into six weeks. I reached out to my the tax preparer to see what was going on and she didn't have an answer for me. She made a few calls, checked the computer, and found out that my return was lost. She filed it again and they told her that there was nothing that she could do differently because my claim was stuck in the system. I could not believe it! What I expected to come in February didn't come until April.

I became increasingly frustrated as I continued to wait for my return. I didn't have money or clients to make it. What was I to do? Yes, unemployment came through but it was only to $238.00 a week. I thought about working Regal Touch in the afternoon and finding a job in the mornings just for income to support my family. I began to have all these mixed emotions on what to do. I started to really question the timing of starting my business. *I don't have money. I don't have business plans and I don't have investors! What was I thinking?*

No, I wasn't thinking at all. I was nuts to start this thing in the beginning. I began to cry because I didn't want to give up on Regal Touch but my girls needed me to be the provider that I had been but I wasn't so sure that the business would let me do that. It's difficult to explain, but as afraid of starting the business as I had been, I was just as afraid to stop it all together. No, I didn't have a college degree to back me up but I knew deep down inside that it was time to be my own boss. Truthfully, I didn't want to work for anyone else ever again.

I had worked in fast food for over 20 years as a manager so I had developed people skills and tough skin. Then working in the administrative field at a desk job, I had learned skills to run a business from a different perspective but even with all of that Regal Touch wasn't up and running as I had imagined. There were nights that I cried and felt like a failure. *I'm too old to be starting over.* It was bad enough that my whole life I had only worked jobs, never really having a career. If I quit a job or was laid off I started all over again. I was tired of starting over.. *Maybe I should send the girls to live with their father until I can get my life together. That would be smart.* I didn't want to have to take my kids and move back home with my parents. I had been out my parents' house since I was eighteen years old. I just couldn't go back. Well, I knew that I could, I just didn't want to go back. It was hard living paycheck to paycheck, making it the best way that we could. I had learned how to survive off the little that we had.

Through the tears, I kept getting up going to meet potential customers. Through all of my mixed emotions, I never let depression kill my destiny. Oh, depression certainly tried to creep in but I had to keep planning and working. I was moving by faith, literally. More often than not, I didn't have the gas money to drive places and market myself, but I went anyway. If I could meet the right people to give my business a chance, it would all be worth it. Yes, I knew that social media could be used as a free marketing tool but I wanted to give a personal touch by meeting potential clients and giving them a true sense of who they would be entrusting their business and homes to. I believed that talking to people face to face would give me the extra edge I needed to gain their business and trust. I wanted to use that added personal touch to set Regal Touch a part from other cleaning services.

Days and weeks went by. Reluctantly, I had started applying for jobs but I still had not gotten a single interview. By this time, Regal Touch had been in operation but there still was not a strong clientele. But, I can gladly say that my family was still intact. We hadn't missed a meal not one day and we were still all together. Yes, times were tough and decisions and concessions had to be made. I cut off the cable because that was a luxury not a necessity. I cooked to save money from eating out and I began to shop in thrift stores. Yeah, I was going through, but there was no need to look busted and defeated at the same time! I started saving money by shopping for bargains. I happily took my bargain finds to the cleaners to be pressed and come out looking brand new. There was no need to spend money that I didn't have just to impress people.

Before I knew it, I was getting more calls for residential cleaning and commercial cleanings. The money was coming in slowly but something at this point was better than none at all. It was like I was making money to get gas for my car and and buy supplies to keep working, that was it. Now, don't get me wrong ,I was excited to be working, I really was, but the money was leaving out of my hands as soon as I made it. I had to figure out how to make the money, manage my resources, and still maintain. I also needed to get more manpower. Up until that point, I had been cleaning mainly by myself but I needed help. It was taking too long for me to clean houses by myself so I hired my brother to help me part time.

Shortly thereafter, I got my first big job. It was quite a memorable experience. The job was considered a move-in cleaning. The client had a huge house that she had yet to move into. She had heard about my business through social media when she posted an inquiry looking for a cleaning service in her local area that was preferably a black owned business. Some ladies in my church had tagged my company and name on her post and I responded. I inboxed the potential customer, introducing myself and letting her know that Regal Touch would love to be of service to her. The customer responded back asking me to come do a walk through at the house the next day.

When I pulled up to the house, I was mesmerized by the size. I was early so I sat outside at least ten minutes before she pulled up. I always try to be timely and have great customer service skills because those two things alone can make or break you in business. Well, while I was waiting, there was a moment of fear that tried to creep in and scare me out of that opportunity. I kept looking at the house and the size alone was frightening. I really didn't know how to tackle the task of cleaning this big house. I hadn't cleaned anything that big before. I let the outside of what it looked like almost hinder me from going in and missing out.

Soon the client arrived and we went inside where she gave me a full walk through of the house. I would be cleaning two levels. The first level consisted of a half bathroom, living room, dining area, kitchen, and a bedroom. Upstairs had three bedrooms and two bathrooms. She wanted the refrigerator and stove cleaned as well as all of the kitchen cabinets. I had read on the internet that when you provide this type of cleaning it's a deep cleaning project and the price should reflect the work that the jobs entails by having a higher cost. Before I could quote her a price, the doorbell rings. It was another cleaning service coming in to quote the customer a price as well. That's when I got nervous because the lady had been talking to me as if I had the job. She continued to tell me her expectations and then asked me how many employees I had and then stated that, she would like to see my business license and insurance as well. At that moment, I was so happy that I had taken the time to place all of my ducks in a row when I started my business. I definitely was legit!

    My only problem was that I didn't actually have an actual crew to help, but I knew my brother was willing to help me out. With confidence, I told her that it would be two of us on the project. She then asked us how long would the job take. Realistically, I didn't have a good answer because I had never had a project that size and I just didn't know how long we needed. Somehow, I came up with a rough estimate of five hours. She asked me to text her my price considering that the other cleaning service representative was standing there. I left feeling like the other person may get the job because they came in a uniform with folder in hand while I had on work scrubs and I took notes in my mind.

    That evening, I received a text from the potential client reminding me to send my price quote and start date if we were to move forward with the project. I gave her my price. My brother and I started two days later. I had 48 hours to come up with cleaning supplies. Cleaning day arrived and we got to the home at 9AM, ready to work. And work we did, but somehow what was supposed to take only five hours to complete turned into 2 days of work. It seemed as if the house was growing while we were working and we were never going to finish! Although the house was basically empty, the deep cleaning took time. We were cleaning everything! Window sills, baseboards, floors, we did it all. While cleaning, I started doubting seriously that this profession was a fit for me. Maybe I really was in over my head. I mean, I knew cleaning took time but according to my research, what I was doing, certainly should not have taken that long. I became more upset and frustrated when I thought about the price that I was charging and the fact we were not able to finish in the allotted time. Not only that but I also felt that I had let my client down. Since, I had already quoted a flat rate there was nothing that I could do to adjust for the extra time. I was locked in to that price that I had originally given to her.

I learned valuable lessons from that job. First, I had grossly underestimated the time needed to complete the task. Secondly, I definitely did not have enough manpower to complete job, which contributed to the time that it took to finish. Lastly, I quoted the wrong price and ultimately undercut myself in the end because I had to pay additional labor costs and spend more on supplies overall.

It was a horrible feeling to call my client and ask her to come lock the house while knowing that I also had to drop the bombshell about the job not being complete. I wish I could have totally skipped that part but I couldn't. When she got to the house I explained to her that the upstairs portion of the house was complete. I also apologized and offered to come back in the morning to complete the job. She went upstairs to review the work. After a few minutes, she called me upstairs and began to tell me a list of things that she did not like and wanted redone. At that moment, honestly I could have cried and actually, later that night I did. I just knew that the eight hours we spent upstairs cleaning was enough. But since I am a woman of my word, I still knew that I had to go back the next day. Unfortunately, now I would have to complete the lower level and redo some things upstairs as well.

We left and drove home and on the ride home all I could do was cry. It was my first big beautiful house and the customer was displeased with everything. I started to doubt myself yet again. I finally composed myself enough to call a friend but as I spoke the tears kept flowing. That friend's response was, "Dry your eyes, go back tomorrow, and fix what the client said was wrong." I begin to complain and say, "But it's not that easy!" The next response from the other end was, " Everything is not created to be easy. Some things are created to be hard in order to teach you a new way of problem solving." That certainly was not what I wanted to hear at that time, but I took the advice and then later that night I prayed that God would give me wisdom and peace because I was feeling like a failure and didn't want to go back to that house to finish or any other house for that matter. Hesitantly, I got up the next morning and went to the store to buy more supplies with the little money that I had.

    I forgot to mention that the client decided to give me a detailed checklist of what she needed done. I couldn't get offended because I had learned from the internet that some companies come with a cleaning checklist when they service a home. The list is meant to protect them and give details as to what was provided while cleaning. At the completion of the service, the customer signs the list verifying that the work was reviewed and completed to satisfaction. In the end, the checklist actually helped us stay on target and to not forget anything.

    Hours roll around and we finally completed the job. I called to let her know to come on back. I just knew we had done a good job. *Everything looks good. She's going to pay me and then I'll be done with this one...finally!* She arrived shortly but she brought her boyfriend with her. Instantly I got nervous. *Why is he here? Here comes another list.* They began to walk through the house and while they're walking, they picked the house apart from level to level and piece by piece. Nothing was cleaned to her satisfaction, well nothing except the carpet, and that was only because we had vacuumed it. I couldn't believe what I was hearing. Certainly there had to be hidden camera somewhere and I was being pranked because this was too much.

Finally, the boyfriend stated that his girlfriend was very anal and a neat freak so nothing was ever clean to her. *Well, what did she hire me for since no one can clean to her satisfaction? She knew she was going to find something wrong from the beginning. Alright, it's late, I'm tired and we've done all that we can do. Now what?* It sounded so good to me in my mind but I knew I couldn't say it like that. So, once again, I gathered myself and explained that I would return and correct any problems that needed attention. Oh, I was hot on the inside! *I have spent more money on gas and brought more supplies only to still leave and go back home without pay. I barely had gas to get here and I was anticipating that money. I had to call a friend and ask to borrow gas money just to get here today.*

I'm borrowing what I don't have yet. I'm never going to make a profit on this job! Clearly you can see that I don't have any clients yet because I was able to come back here three times with no need for schedule adjustments. Instead of really saying what was on my mind, I agreed to come back again. However, before I left, I took notes and wrote down everything she told me that was wrong.

That night I started looking up ways to clean the trouble spots. There were all types of videos on how to clean stains in different areas of a house. The next day, I took my notes from the videos I had watched, her complaint list, made adjustments to the cleaning supplies that the videos suggested based on the supplies that I already had because I definitely could not afford to buy anymore, and I pieced together a cleaning crew to provide more manpower. We were able to complete the job in a reasonable amount of time and we got paid! I wasn't expecting a tip or anything based on the issues that had transpired. At that point, I was just happy to get paid.

In hindsight, I can see that there was a lesson to be learned from that experience. That experience was a teachable moment that was preparing me to deal with different personalities, pricing, staffing issues, supplies, time management, among other things. Yes, she was very anal with some of her requests but she was in fact paying for a service that she believed would meet her expectation. It took some time, but I took into account the things that she said. I looked at the situation from her perspective, stopped playing the victim role, and then made the adjustments to provide my client with the service that she expected. The process was definitely tedious and nerve-racking but in the end it helped to produce a better and more excellent standard of quality service from Regal Touch.

5

WHEN TRAGEDY HITS

Regal Touch Maid & Cleaning Services was growing. I was seeing multiple clients weekly instead of just three clients a month. I was really starting to believe in my business more and the results of my hard work were starting to show. My clientele list had expanded and now included beauty shops, barber shops, business offices, and churches.

I had finally increased my marketing techniques. I created social media pages to gain more exposure and I started sending flyers out as well. I even paid for my ads to run and circulate on certain social media sites so that I could expand to an even larger group of people. Eventually, my social media marketing began to pay off and I landed a client on the west side of Chicago.

My new client was a pastor of a church. He contacted me because he wanted his church cleaned for an upcoming event that he was hosting. The notice was a little late but Regal Touch was able to get the church cleaned and smelling good before his event started. The pastor was so impressed by the work that he asked Regal Touch to come every two weeks. I was super excited because he was my very first bi-weekly client. It was quite the drive to take every two weeks but I did it, rain sleet or snow. I remained faithful to it and never once complained but it really did became a test of my endurance to see it through. However, I have learned that It's best to be faithful over the few things that you do have then to complain about big things you still don't have.

Doors were continuously opening for me insomuch that people were still gifting and sowing into my business. People continued to give me referrals and share my business flyers. I even had people give me cleaning supplies. I was overwhelmed with the support and encouragement that I received. Now although, business was increasing, I still had to fine tune my marketing strategy for a target audience. At this point, I had just been trying to get clients and although I did have an idea of the clientele that I wanted, I still hadn't solidified my approach.

One thing I had to learn more about was my target audience. Everyone didn't need cleaning services but some people did. Who exactly are those people? That list may include wives who work and don't have time to clean and cook once they get home; single businessmen on the go, who get up and leave out early and come home late; and single men and women who may need help monthly to maintain housekeeping. The more I learned about my audience the better I would be able to market to their needs. Even finding the right commercial properties were important. I had to know that market as well. I had to know what other business owners needed to help them better focus on other aspects of their business while leaving the cleaning aspect to me.

I also learned that the market service area of a business is very important. I decided to market my business in both Indiana and Illinois. I lived in Indiana but to crossover into Illinois was only a ten minute drive for me therefore it definitely made sense to capture a larger service market. However, a downside was trying to set boundaries for the exact market area and price accordingly to reflect the pricing of area comparisons. Ultimately, I would have to either charge the same price across the board or change the price based on the state. I noticed very quickly that in higher income areas my prices were very low in comparison to competitors which has both advantages and disadvantages. I knew it was bad when clients would make comments like, "You're prices are really cheap, your work is worth more than you're charging." Although, they were complimenting my service, it once again reminded me that I was selling myself short in regard to the value that I bring as a person and now as a business owner. If I didn't see the service as being worth more than the client wouldn't either. Reality hit me. I still had to change my perception.

    I was uncertain and reluctant to change my prices because I didn't want to lose the clientele that I had or scare away any potential clients. I realized that many of the inquiry calls I was receiving were actually other businesses calling around for different quotes to see what the market rates were. After debating with myself, I reassessed my value and reconfigured some of my pricing. I was content to know that no matter what, there were people out there who needed the services that I provided and would be willing to pay the prices that I set.

    Another thing I had to consider was travelling expenses. I had to justify the compensation and make allotments for distance, manpower, gas prices, etc. I'll be honest though, in the very beginning, I didn't care too much about the "extra" factors. I was just happy to be working. Indiana had a lower tax bracket than Illinois so everything was cheaper in Indiana. However, I also learned that in both states, there were some areas that had a rather large customer base for cleaning services so those services were highly sought after. In the end, I decided to keep the price the same for both states. A lot of people told me that I was in over my head by covering two states at once. In fact, according to some, it wasn't a realistic idea for a new business. Truthfully, nothing about the beginnings of Regal Touch was realistic or textbook. I had been operating from a point of faith, personal research, determination, and hard work. Despite the naysayers, Regal Touch carried on and wherever there was a request for cleaning I went.

I had received so much help for Regal Touch already that I didn't harp on not having things. I just used what I had to make things happen. As I stated before, one of my first clients gifted me a photo shoot. He wanted to sow into my business and help it grow. What I didn't mention was the horror story that surrounded the photo shoot. In fact, let me offer a disclaimer to you. Please be advised that as a business owner, you are subject to good days with great stories and bad days with horror stories. With that being said, let me give you the scoop of the photo shoot horror story. Well, let me recant my statement. The photo shoot itself was a great experience! It was just surrounded by a series of bad events that tried to damper the experience.

The day of the photo shoot I was too excited! I had gotten my hair done and some clothes custom made. I just knew this was a great opportunity to help my business brand and marketing. *These pictures are going to be a great marketing tool! People will be able to associate a face with the company name.* I drove to the site where I would be getting my makeup done before going to the photo gallery. My vehicle at that time was a sedan and it sat rather low to the ground. Well those that know anything about Chicago knows that the city has many potholes and speed bumps that will destroy your car if you're not careful while driving. Well, that particular day, I remember hitting a speed bump and saying, "geesh, that didn't feel too good" but I kept going.

I arrived at my destination, got out of my car, and then looked under the hood. I didn't see anything leaking underneath and everything looked fine so I gathered my things to go inside and get my makeup done. A few hours passed and then it was time to leave and go to the photo gallery. I got in the car and it wouldn't start. I kept trying but it wouldn't start. What could be wrong? I had never had that problem before. My car was only a few years old. I kept an oil change and regular maintenance done. I sat there and the tears started flowing again. I sat there on total disbelief. I just couldn't believe that I was having that sort of issue on such an important day. I was ashamed to tell someone that it wouldn't start, but I also didn't know what to do. My options were to either sit there and miss the photo shoot opportunity or make a move.

As I sat there, I noticed that everyone was walking out and getting in cars to leave. I had to think fast. I got out my car and flagged down a lady on her way to her car and asked her for a ride. She had been in the makeup studio with me . She graciously said yes. I was happy that she didn't ask questions because I was too embarrassed and devastated to talk about what was going on. I knew that if I cried any more my makeup would have been ruined, my spirit crushed, and my determination gone. I couldn't let anything get in the way of this blessing so I decided to deal with the aftermath of my car situation later. I will admit that the whole time that I rode in the car with her, I kept thinking that the entire situation was a dream. This had to be a joke for real. There was no way that I had gotten all the way to Chicago on such an important day and my car decided to call it quits with no notice. That sort of thing only happens in movies.

The more that I thought about my car, the more problems came to my mind. There was no way that I could be without a vehicle, especially when business had finally started picking up. I had to figure out how to get my car from Chicago back to Indiana. I didn't have any extra money. I had used what little I had to prepare for the photo shoot. Somehow, I went on with a smile to the photo shoot. Looking back, I'm glad I persevered despite what was going on because that moment taught me how to survive when tragedy hits. Do I fold or keep moving? Well, I made some calls to get a ride home and to get my car towed back to Indiana. Thankfully, I had a friend available to come to my rescue. Unfortunately, he didn't know what the problem was either but he did help me get it towed back to a shop in Indiana.

I failed to mention that this happened on a Friday. The weekends were particularly busy for me and all I could think about was how to keep going for the weekend. I had to wait until Monday to see what was wrong. In the midst of waiting, I prayed and went through that weekend moving about with the help of my support team. It's so important to have positive people around you. They help drown out the negative noise that wants to overtake you.

Up until that point, I hadn't realized that there were people waiting in the background for me to fail. All weekend I heard comments like, "How are you going to see clients now? Maybe you should drop this and get a regular job." My mind was made up and whether someone believed in me or not, I believed in myself! The negative Nancy's only gave me fuel to keep pushing harder and to trust God through the process.

I started figuring out a backup plan to get to customer that week. No matter what was going on I always had the faith to believe that everything I was going through was to take me to a place of success. By the end of the week, the mechanic informed me that my engine had died. I asked him how much a new engine would cost and the price of any associated fees. The price he quoted shook me a tad bit. Then I called the dealership because I had a warranty. They went back and forth with me for two weeks and then concluded that my warranty was good. I was relieved to know that my car would be repaired. Well, a few days later they called back and told me that because I took the car to an outside mechanic, my warranty was invalid. According to them, they had no proof that the mechanic had not tampered with the engine .I was out of luck.

I hung up the phone and once again sat in total shock

and disbelief. What was I going to do now? My entire business was based on traveling to clients homes and properties. I instantly begin to doubt myself yet again. *This can't be what God has for me. The process is too hard. I'm going through too much. The transition is harder each day. It seems as if the more I grow, the more things happen.* Business was getting stable to the point that I had clients on the calendar each week. Things had really taken a positive turn and then my car messes up.

I continued to mull over my dilemma and then I began to see that I was depending on myself more than God. I was too busy being the victim and not seeing how victorious I really was. I had started Regal Touch with no business plan, no money, no loans, and no investors. However, time had gone by and my girls and I hadn't missed a meal, we had a roof over our head, and until my engine decided to clonk out, I had been driving my car. God had provided for us for four months even though things had been tight so surely this car wasn't too big of a problem for Him to handle. So, I dried my tears, got up from my pity party, and started thinking about the next course of action. I came up with a plan to borrow a vehicle until I was able to get a new one. I was determined to not to let my transportation issues stop my business from growing.

My plan included me setting my pride aside and asking for help once again. Members of my family allowed me to use their cars and I scheduled my appointment times around the availability of cars. Now let me clarify myself by saying that you want to have pride in your business. However, you do not want to be prideful in such a way to think that "you" are all that is needed to run a successful business. At some point, everyone needs someone other than oneself. However, it is often difficult to ask for help when people don't believe in your vision and are waiting on you to fail. I had been through too many bad times and didn't know how much resilience I had left. Ultimately, I had to overcome my feelings and keep going. If you don't remember anything else in this book, remember that you must keep going! One monkey definitely does not stop the show.

Listen, I had to come to terms that I can't do everything on my own and I will need help. So what if people know that I don't have a car anymore! As long as I could get to work and make money that's all that mattered. I keep saying it because it's true, you must look at your problems from different views. That's the only way to stay focused and persevere.

Another part of my plan was to follow-up with the IRS. I reached out to them and they never gave me a clear date of when I would be receiving my return. I knew that if I could just get my tax return I could buy a truck. Even while waiting, I had to laugh at myself because I remembered the times that I complained about my car being too small because I couldn't get vacuum cleaners in it. Well, now I didn't have that problem because I didn't have a car at all. Maybe I could use this waiting period and specify that I needed a truck and not a car.

Before I knew it, weeks were rolling by. I was getting to work and getting my girls to school. It was as if I never missed a beat. In fact, work was picking up. I knew that if I could get through this rough patch, I could achieve anything. I started to develop a "let's make it happen" attitude.

Finally, my return came and I was able to purchase a truck. What a relief! Now the calls were coming in like I had prayed for. The only thing was that I needed some more manpower to complete the work that was coming in. My brother and I were working from sunup to sundown. There were many days that I would be so tired that my feet and hands would swell up.

My only off was Sundays. However, Sundays weren't actually "off days" because I was a faithful and active member of my church. I know that some may not believe in God but I do and I realize that He gives me strength and I feel revived when I go to church. Now, I must admit there were moments that I didn't feel like going to church not because I didn't believe God would bless my business with Regal Touch. I just got tired of people asking me questions about Regal Touch and watching to see how I would react given the challenges often presented by new business ventures. It was hard going through the process publicly. There are always people watching to see you fail and others to see if you practice what you preach.

Many days, I would walk into my local assembly and be dog tired but I knew people were watching me. That's when I decided that even through my struggle, there would still be a testimony. I was confident that many people would get excited with me when once they saw how God would bless Regal Touch. God was using me to be a example for others to see if I could make it through tough times, they could too!. If I could start a business with nothing and it multiplied into three times more than expected for a first year business, my struggle would definitely worth the watch.

6

BOSSING UP

As business calls picked up so did the amount of work. I needed help. But it was difficult to pay my brother for helping, so how was I supposed to hire a staff? Yes, my brother is family but I appreciated his help and he deserved to be compensated for his work. I believe in doing things right and I wanted to have integrity in my business dealings. I knew that if I started my business with integrity my name would be known to be good among men. I needed to hire additional help and very quickly at that. I knew that I couldn't pay much but I also didn't expect people to work for pennies.

 I was still trying to figure out how to go about getting staff when God sent someone to ask me for a job. She was very forthcoming when I met her and she expressed that she was willing to take whatever I could afford to pay her because she wasn't working and just needed some type of income. Well, just like she felt that the job was a help to her, she was a help to me. We needed the help and it was right on time. I figured she was an older lady, so she probably knew something about cleaning. After checking her background history, the rest I thought would be easy.

 We began to discuss the job and as we were talking, the

lady began to ask some questions. One question was about pay. She wanted to know how much I paid an hour. I really wasn't sure how to answer that question or some of the other questions that she had, so I told her that I would get back to her. In the meantime, I looked up information on minimum wage. I was shocked to learn how low it really was! In fact, the minimum wage made me determined to offer employees a much better wage than the minimum. In regard to her question about hours, I was stuck on that one too! I was stunned because until then I hadn't thought about the fact that not too many people are willing to work from sun up until sun down. In fact, asking someone to work those type of hours is actually unfair and unreasonable.

The more I thought about things, the more I realized that all of the questions that she was asking were legitimate questions. I just had never figured the part of my business out. Up until that point I had just been running things off the top of my head. I had no structure and I certainly didn't have employment paperwork for potential employees to complete. I should have been better prepared for what was ahead for my business. Surely I knew that at some point I would need to hire staff. Why hadn't I thought about working hours, wages, and possible benefits? Honestly, I had thought about those things, however, I had never implemented a plan to make things work. I had underestimated the planning process and the administrative role of an entrepreneur.

There was a lot of administration that I needed done but I wasn't able to sit down and get it accomplished, especially after business had increased. I knew Regal Touch was growing and I needed to learn to maintain everything until I could afford help. However, the truth of the matter was that I wasn't going to get far with Regal Touch until I slowed down and put some policies and procedures together.

A huge part of the policies and procedures that I needed to implement dealt with the different types of cleaning and the instruction of how to properly execute the cleaning processes. It is important for any business to have training procedures and policies in place to ensure that there is a standard of work and a method to get things completed. For Regal Touch, it was imperative that I trained my employees on methods and techniques for both residential and commercial properties. I started by doing much of the training while using a hands on approach. As a new business with a small staff it is often quite effective for the owner to be found working side by side with the staff. That approach can build unity and respect for an employer-employee relationship and it can also be beneficial to the customer because there is often more trust of the work being done more efficiently when the business owner is present.

As a business owner, you set the standard, tone, and pace for your business. You determine the core values of your company and after a while customer preferences and feedback are interjected to help create a great customer experience. In my area of business, there were things that needed to be considered such as the difference between surface cleaning and thorough cleaning, residential versus commercial cleaning, etc. In other words, whatever service you provide needs to have a structure to it. It is not always wise to operate without a plan and it is most certainly a disservice to yourself and future employees to not have policies in place to provide a framework of expectations. Yes, you as a business owner may know what you want, how you want it done, and when it's scheduled to be done, however, you are more effective when using managerial skills to convey all of those ideas to those who work with you and ultimately for you.

Even with the ideas that I did have and the help that I was receiving, at times, it still wasn't enough. Most business take three years to establish recurring clients but I was still in my first year of business when that started to happen for me. I found myself becoming increasingly overwhelmed, stressed, and tired. It seemed like I never had a day off and business was picking up to the point that my only two employees were working with no days off. I wasn't trying to overwork them because I needed them. So, because I was feeling bad for my employees, I started doing extra jobs by myself to give them off days. One would think to hire more people, however, at the time it wasn't the best option because money wasn't consistent enough.

Because of the nature of my business, I typically received some amount of money daily. That was a good thing but it also became difficult to to keep my financial books. I was paying people, buying supplies and purchasing gas almost daily. Admittedly, I wasn't taking the time to keep track of my operating costs. It was so easy to just spend and expect more the next day.

Well, the money was expected daily but unfortunately it wasn't always received daily as expected. This was especially true in instances where customers would cancel on me. Cancellations were another lesson to learn in business. If I didn't attach a cancellation fee to the service contracts, people wouldn't care about canceling appointments and wasting my time. Usually, money has a way of getting people's attention. It took a while to learn that my time is valuable and that I should charge accordingly. It was frustrating to schedule client appointments thinking that you were going to get paid only later to receive a text message stating that the client had changed their mind.

I can recall a time that I had three cancellations in one week. I was devastated. I had been so excited for that week of work because it was very rare that I was booked every day. Once I received the cancellations, I had to tell my workers. Telling my staff about the cancellation was embarrassing because they were depending on that money too. In the moment, it was like I was afraid to communicate with customers because I didn't want their business going anywhere else. I was answering calls and text messages at all times of the night. I would let clients change their schedules last minute and I even let someone pay me late. Now, that I can look back on the situation, I caused a lot of problems for myself

I mentioned this before but I'm going to say it again. It is important to value your product and work. For a long time, I had been letting anything go just to have clients. It was like a bad relationship where I let a man do whatever he wanted to me as long as he stayed with me. Regal Touch was becoming that way early on in business relationships. It hit home to me when I had a chance to go do a walkthrough for an industrial company. The company was looking for a cleaning service to do basic cleaning. I was so elated to even be asked to come by and view the potential project that I let the excitement cloud my better judgment. They were moving into a warehouse and needed the offices cleaned out and the bathrooms detailed cleaned.

I remember walking through the site thinking, "Lord this a lot of work. Can we handle this? "The place was filthy and covered in layers of dirt. The bathrooms had been out of order for so long that the smell was unbearable to say the least. Once the walkthrough was compete, the gentlemen asked me my price to take on the project. The project was both large and intensive. They wanted walls washed down, baseboards cleaned, plus sweeping and mopping. It was three huge offices and two bathrooms total. I knew that I needed more manpower. As I processed the numbers and timing my head, I was estimating that the complete job would be finished within 10 (ten) days. Of course out of my mouth proceeded something totally different. I shocked myself when I said that in two days all of the work would be done. Next, I head myself quote a price and the man looked at me as to say, "you can't be serious."

From his expression, I thought he meant that my price was too high but he looked at me and said, "I think you should add another zero to that amount." I had grown so accustomed to cleaning for pennies that I didn't know what it was to receive dollars. He said to me, "If you don't know your worth, no one else will. Then you will always be treated cheaper than you really are."

    I left there and got in my car and cried...again. This whole self-worth issue in my personal life kept creeping up in my business affairs. I thought I had confronted the issue and made amends but obviously I hadn't completed the process. I had to find a balance that allowed me to remain humble yet confident in my abilities. Truthfully, I wasn't certain of how to accomplish that because for so long I felt that I always had to downplay my ideas for others. It seemed like I was always the one who would cancel my plans to go along with someone else's. I had to get it together. It was years later and I found myself operating a business and still taking whatever was offered to appease others. I took that teachable moment as another reminder to step up and stand up.

    Weeks passed and I made a decision to reach out to a business support group that I had discovered while browsing social media. The group consisted of women who were entrepreneurs focused on collaboration, sharing, and gaining information to further business. I visited the group during one the group's meetings and that night change my life for the better. Everyone was creative, sincere, and ambitious like myself. We all had a common goal which was to start a business, grow a business, and be successful running a business. I needed this support system to help me grow and build a brand out of Regal Touch.

    It was so much information in the first meeting that I had been ignorant to. I knew I had a long way to go but I was willing to get there. I have always had friends that supported me and I found this group to be an extension of my core group of friends. The business group was impactful. It seemed as if everyone in the group was starting from the ground and working themselves up. The leader of the group was so encouraging and knowledgeable and what she didn't know she researched and brought people in to teach us.

Having accountability partners that we would talk to weekly was also a strength of the group. As accountability partners, the goal was to check on each other and make sure that we were working on our businesses. It felt good having an accountability partner committed to checking on Regal Touch and rooting for growth and success. We even received daily encouragement messages to help us fight through challenges. Although, I was the only one in the group that had fully started a business, I found myself soaking up all the information that I could during our monthly meetings. I needed this group for Regal Touch because when I had questions there were more people around to help me out.

Let me take a moment to further explain how vital it is to have an accountability partner. Those people help you grow. Do not get a partner that will agree with everything you say. Get someone that is able to pull you out of a rut when you stuck, not someone that will get in the rut with you and roll around in pity for you. It's good to have people around with questions. "That's a good idea but you may need to rethink it." Is that profitable for the business? What resources do you have to back it up? All of that is good to hear. Everyone who says "No" is not hating on you or your ideas. How about thinking of "No" as a clear indication that it's just not a good idea and you can do better. I found myself encouraged daily by this group of awesome go getters that I had connected with. I never felt left out and I didn't perceive a hint of jealousy or envy from them. Everything was genuine and it was easy for me to take correction and ideas from them.

It's crucial that you watch who you share your vision and dreams with. I noticed that everyone can't handle the visions you have for yourself and business. Just because someone is a personal friend that doesn't necessarily make them good for business. It's ok to have friend just for business, the ones who have vision and can understand your crazy ideas and see creativity in them. It's good to have friends that understand business life and it's also good to have associates that offer nothing more than good conversation. Those were the types of relationships that I developed with my business support group. We become close and celebrated the growth and change in our businesses.

Having support is needed but it doesn't always come when you want it or who you expect it from. I have always been the one to support the dreams and visions of other people. I'm the one who supports your event and buys a ticket. If you are making pies, I'll buy one. If you are singing, I'll come to your recording. I've never had an issue with supporting others. With my cleaning business, I knew that my support wouldn't necessarily come from people that I know actually making appointments with me. Everyone doesn't need a house cleaning appointment with Regal Touch in order to support me. I get it. Sometimes, my support came from simple things like sharing my flyer on social media or tagging me in referrals when people were looking for a cleaning service.

Now don't get me wrong, it was great having support from my new business group but I was expecting to get support from some people that I had supported along the way. Where were those people? Well, during prayer I was reminded that people aren't obligated to support me in the same manner that I support them. By nature, I am an encourager, motivator, and support system for others to lean on. A lot of people that I support need me in more ways than I need them, and I'm learning to be okay with that fact. I cannot base the support that I give on that amount of support that I receive.

Business continued to rapidly grow and I was excited about it. Yes, the struggle was real and days of tears where frequent but I never lost hope in Regal Touch. I saw myself becoming a better strategist as I continued to seek wisdom. Wisdom as a business owner is so vital to your growth and development. Quickly, I had to learn that every door that was opening was not meant for me to go through it. Some doors opened to teach me ways to handle certain situations if and when they would arise.

I had an experience where a major opportunity was presented to me to provide services for a three story office building. The project called for janitorial cleaning in the common areas only and the public restrooms on each floor. I had gone into the building to provide services for a beauty salon and I met the building manager while I was on my way to the salon. I had my cleaning supplies with me and the manager began to ask me questions about my business. Next, thing I knew, the manager asked me when would I be able to start cleaning the entire building because their cleaning person had stopped coming in.

The assignment called for overnight cleaning. I was given keys to the building and as long as I kept the building clean, my schedule was up to me. I went alone because I was trying to keep all of the profit for myself (bad idea) instead of having at least one other person assist to make the job more manageable. The building had security cameras and a police officers who would always sit around outside. I was comfortable with the environment but to my surprise, the outside of the building was safer than the inside. There was a lot more activity in the building than I had expected. The building was comprised of doctor offices on the first two floors and the third floor housed beauty salons and barber shops only. People were going in and out of there late night and everyone who rented a space in the building had a key. In fact, I would lock the doors while working inside because I never knew who would be moving about the building.

I look back now and can say that I truly believe that I had angels watching me because I never feared being alone in the building. Even so, I had friends that were concerned about me being alone at night so they often called and checked on me throughout the night.

I'll never forget an incident I went through at that building that made me say, "all money ain't good money." One night I came in through the front doors like my usual routine and the hallway was trashed. I had never seen it like that before. There was a strong smell of liquor and you could see the bottles by the trash can. Well, the barbershop on the third floor was having a party. There were people everywhere throughout the building. I was upset because they were making my job harder by trashing the place. I decided to clean the first and second floors and then head upstairs when the partying was over. Some time had passed and I thought everyone was gone so I rode the elevator to the third floor to start cleaning. When I got off the elevator, I was shocked at what I saw. There was trash everywhere. It was as if they had the actual party in the hallways. To make the matter worse, the bathrooms were horrific.

I was in the ladies restroom cleaning up and a drag queen came in to use the bathroom. I was startled to say the least! Not so much because it was a drag queen, although I'll be honest and say that I was caught off guard by the appearance, however, I was more surprised because I thought that everyone had left the building. Well, she was intoxicated and begin to urinate all over the floor. I couldn't believe that someone would see you cleaning and be that rude. I was furious! I spoke up and said, " Excuse me, but the toilet is right over there or you could've gone to the men's bathroom in the first place."

Now admittedly, that last part of my comment may not have been the nicest things to say, but I just couldn't get myself together as I watched what had just happened. Angrily, she turned around looked at me and said, "You're just the maid. You're here to pick up after people." She then proceeded to walk out of the bathroom, laughing all the way down the hall, and kicking trash as she went along. That was the first time that I really felt like "the help". I didn't feel respected at all for the work that I was doing. Did I really need this money this bad? Or was I trying to hold on to it because I had bragged about getting my first commercial property building?

Sometimes the hassle of doing things is not worth it if you are afraid or in danger while doing it. Sometimes saving face can cost you your face! However, I want to encourage you to never let shame dictate you from moving forward. I have come to the realization that not sticking with something doesn't make me a failure. It's not trying at all, that makes you a failure! I stayed with that cleaning project as long as I could because I needed the money. It was consistent and I never had issues getting paid. It just wasn't safe. Sadly even knowing that I stayed. I guess I didn't have enough sense to leave, so after while another door presented itself....they got rid of me themselves.

Out of the blue, one day the owner told that me I was too high in price and that I would have to lower my price or she would find a cheaper cleaning woman. I took that as a sign to leave. Safety was more important than a dollar anyway. What's the use of making money that if I'm dead, I won't get to spend anyway? So, I gave the keys back and walked out of there wondering what was next. One of the most valuable lessons learned from that experience was the importance of having a contract for the services that I provide. If I had a contact in place, they would of had to keep me or pay me out of the contract.

As the business continued to go through changes, I did my best to continue to balance motherhood. My eldest daughter was graduating from high school during the first year of my business, so I had to provide additional support for things such as prom and graduation. Being a single mother had always been a financial struggle for me but I never let it get to me. I gave my girls what I could and made sure that they was clean, clothed, and fed. No, we didn't have it all but what I had I gave it to them with all that I could. So, if owning my own business could give my girls a better life than me working hard and dealing with the bumps and bruises of business was not in vain. I had to keep pressing based on that fact alone.

My daughters were old enough to understand some of the things that were going on and they often offered me support and encouragement. Even so, in my heart, I was ashamed that we had to go through the process of rebuilding our lives as I struggled with unemployment and then owning and operating a business start-up. Through the process we went through a lot of changes. However, I often reflect on things now, and I am glad that things happened the way that they did.

My business started during a time that my daughters were at a very impressionable age. I worked hard to present myself as a hard worker. I didn't want them so caught up in pop culture and the media and see every way to get money, except the right way. Yes, I knew that they were getting teased because their mom was the cleanup lady. I would tell them that as long as long as I was making an honest living and providing for them, let people talk. Sadly, I learned from my girls and from hearing comments firsthand, that it wasn't just kids that would say negative stuff about my career choice. Grown-ups talked about me too. I have heard all sorts of comments and questions including, "Black people were freed from slavery and being maids, and here you go being a maid." "Do you feel ashamed going in people's home and cleaning up behind them?" Well my answer to that question was and still is very simple. "No. I am not ashamed of what I do. It's an honest living and I enjoy it. I'm a boss!"

7

STARTED FROM THE BOTTOM NOW I'M HERE

Nobody had taught me anything about the business that I was in. I had landed here by accident! One night I decided to have a moment of self-reflection. As always, I had questions to answer. *Do I want to clean all my life? Do I want to own it and hire someone to run it for me? Am I passionate about cleaning or was this a quick fix for my situation?* Those were just a few of the questions that I had. Every now and then it's important to review your "Why"! I knew that I was blessed to have a growing business but did I see myself as having it for the long haul? These questions were not uncommon to be asking this early in business. I knew that eventually if I wanted to be successful and have longevity some more things would have to change. It was time that I started to think and act like a businesswoman and carry myself accordingly. Yes, I own a cleaning service but I needed people to see more than that. I needed people to see a businesswoman on the rise.

Now it was time to know my purpose for Regal Touch! How was Regal Touch helping me fulfill my destiny? Yes, it's a cleaning service but I had so many ideas about expanding into different areas beyond the normal cleaning service. However, in thinking about some of these new ventures, I had to do some evaluations. *Was I strong enough to handle running a service* business that could potentially turn into a million dollar business?

Regal Touch had now become my career. How Regal Touch would grow going forth would be a result of drive, determination, and motivation. It looks and sounds cute saying I'm a boss but being a boss carries weight! As an owner, or a boss, people are watching and waiting to see if you are all talk and no show. I didn't realize the amount of many people that were watching Regal Touch until I started receiving inbox messages on social media. People would send encouraging text messages. Simple messages like, "I'm watching you; You are inspiring me to open a business; Write a book" were greatly appreciated. It was like God would have people send these messages to encourage me to keep pushing. I realized that I had been so busy that I hadn't taken time to reflect on what I was actually doing.

I had a legit, successful, and expanding business that had been birthed from a moment of despair and now ran based on faith, hard work, and ambition. I would run into people on the streets and people would let me know they had been watching me and were rooting for my success. I knew then that I could no longer let the title of "boss" be bigger than the work that I was putting in. I didn't want Regal Touch being an ordinary small black owned business. I was preparing my mind to think ten years into the future.

It was time that I got a handle on the back end of my business. All though I was out in the field making money, I still didn't have policies and procedures in place for Regal Touch. Administration was a weak point in Regal Touch. I had mishandled so many things on the administrative side of my business. I needed to get my house in order! Now that business was growing, companies were asking me for my insurance papers, worker's compensation information, etc. Commercial properties began asking me to send proposals. I had to learn how to bid for jobs, how to respond to emails for jobs, learn to schedule employees for weekly work, etc. .It was hard cleaning, answering phone calls and text messages, and booking appointments without forgetting. There were days that I would get home and forget to write employees hours down for the work that they had done that day. I would forget to call customers back about potential service. As much as I needed an administrative assistant, I still couldn't afford to pay one. So it was time for me to figure out a strategy to get things done without losing potential customers in the process. It was time to stop making excuses and to start executing.

My business operations were rapidly going from weekly projects to daily projects and I had to adjust. There was no more just simply getting the job done and getting paid. The stakes were getting higher and I needed to know how to successfully run business and not run away from it.

I decided to use my resources and I started by asking my accountability group for help in these areas that I was lacking in. The advice they offered was extremely helpful. Among their advice was different resources that I could use to help me stay organized. There were scheduling apps to help me keep up with potential clients and different apps that could help me create forms I needed while on the go. I even leaned that I could hire a virtual assistant, someone who could do all of my administrative work from a computer all while living in another state. Virtual assistants were cheaper than normal administrative assistants who would come into the office from nine to five.

There were so many things was out there I could use to help my business run more efficiently. The only downfall was that I needed consistency. By now you would think that I would know the true definition of consistency. The truth is that I knew routine and my routine was in shambles. I knew I couldn't keep operating like this and expect to be a profitable business in the next three to five years. Something had to change! Regal Touch was growing but needed more than just properties and a bigger cleaning crew. It was time to step up and brand Regal Touch. I needed to get my business to a point that it wouldn't need me doing everything in order to operate sufficiently. The true end game of business is to make money work even when you're not physically working. Surviving in the world today takes multiple streams of income. In fact, most millionaires have at least seven streams of income. So it was time for me to think like that as well. No more just cleaning as usual but it's time to make Regal Touch one of the best amongst its competitors.

Even with the growth, I made it my point to be aware of what my competitors were doing. I wanted to know what they were doing and how they were doing it. I needed to gauge their service and find ways to be better, keep my current clientele, and reach out to potential clients as well. It might sound strange, but I loved getting clients that had used a cleaning service before. I saw their feedback as invaluable. It was my chance to find out what other cleaning services didn't do right. I'll never forget a client telling me that she caught her previous cleaning service cleaning with bleach wipes in her bathroom. I couldn't believe that someone would be bold enough to clean with wet wipes.

My employees and I were scrubbing on hands and knees and people were out here cleaning houses within two hours or less with wet wipes. We were out here giving thorough cleaning services from top to bottom while other cleaning services were taking the quick way out. From that conversation, I could see how some cleaning services were known for their speed.

I also had a client tell me that the cleaning service used before had broken her microwave and then blamed it on her. I was appalled. One of the biggest things I teach my employees is that if something was already broken or broke while Regal Touch was cleaning, report it immediately!!! I believe in reporting every little detail and documenting accordingly.. I had to find out the hard way that everyone is not honest and if they can blame you for damaging something that was already broken and get you to pay for it or you offer them a free service as compensation, they will. I had heard so many horror stories about cleaning services that if I could help it I didn't want Regal to add to the horror story library. Regal Touch's job is to leave clients with the best experience possible so that they will forget the others and continue to go with us. Regal Touch was about giving royalty treatment in all aspects from customer service to excellency cleaning services.

I will be the first to admit that it does get difficult at times to give great customer service when the customer isn't always the nicest. Buy hey, that's the way of business. Everyone will not be nice and accepting but that is ok! Be confident in who you are and what you bring to the industry. During my time as a business owner, I have faced rejection due to my race and gender. It seemed as if the odds were stacked up against me in so many areas. Nevertheless, I have never let someone else's issues stop me from doing business and doing it to the best of my ability. From day one, I made it my mission to provide good customer service, be timely, consistent, and offer quality cleaning experiences. To a lot of people, it's virtually impossible to see a full year in business because most people fold from the pressure.

But then again, there are people like me, still standing admittedly some days stronger than others, but determined nonetheless to never fall down and stay there.

Another part of my reflection showed that I needed to have more publicity. Several people shared stories with me about how networking events introduced them to potential clients. So after mulling over the prospects, I decided to get the ball rolling and attend some networking events that could possibly help Regal Touch grow. I went through a season of attending different workshops on business tools and ideas. I figured that the best way to grow was to learn and also get around others who were where I was trying to go in business.

I have always been one to love hands on teaching methods because it has always been easy for me to learn while working. I believe that's a factor as to why I'm finding success. I love hands on work. Those networking events were giving me the power and push I needed to survive. I would be so empowered hearing others talk about their journey with their business. I recall sitting in an event with business women. These women were CEO of their companies, had been in business a number of years, and some had even been on television shows. I was so impressed with their transparency of how they got to the place of success. I truly believe that some of the best research material is that of another's story. Especially, when you get a chance to pick someone's brain with questions. Unlike some people, I don't have a problem letting someone know that I don't know something. I'm willing to learn from whomever I can to move Regal Touch ahead no matter what race, religion, or color the person I'm learning from maybe.. Money is green!

Wisdom also told me find some business classes to attend, classes that catered to entrepreneurs. Ironically, there was such a class right in my neighborhood. The class met for eight weeks, one night a week for three hours. It was geared to teaching basic principles of business and once the class was completed you would leave with a business plan. I knew the business plan was important because from experience people would ask me about it when I mentioned that I needed a loans or investors. I finally had realized the importance of having a business plan but I'm glad not having one didn't hinder Regal Touch from existing.

The class was so empowering and eye opening. Every week I wanted to learn more and do more with my business because of the information that I obtained in class. I loved the class because it was full of aspiring business owners, some who had started like me. We all were striving to get to the same goal, and that goal was to be successful business owners. The teacher of the class had thirty years of experience with two successful businesses that she owned. I felt like even though I had started Regal Touch without a business plan and without any plans at all, this class was my next level for business. The more I learned, the more I realized that there was a lot that I didn't know. Despite my uneasiness, I never let it stop me from learning what I needed for the next level of business.

8

BALANCE

As a business owner, is there a such thing as balance? How do I deal with motherhood, marketplace, and ministry? Those were some of the questions that were on my mind but the real question behind all of that was how can I be successful and not miss a beat? I have always stayed busy in life. I have always served others and I often went out of my way to be faithful in whatever I did. Consistency has always been important to me in my life. I had to learn by the age of 19 years old the importance of providing for someone other than myself. I was a teenage mother who found out early in life that you can't blame anyone for what you don't have. You have to get out and work for it, if you want it. So working hard wasn't new to me; it was in my blood. I always worked hard for others but had never really seen the fruit of my labor to the point where I was proud of myself.

Ministry had increased for me a year prior to creating Regal Touch. I remember having a conversation with God and asking Him questions. I knew He was calling me to a higher position but I was hesitant. *Can I handle it? Do you trust me to be a senior leader in my church? I'm not worthy.* Despite my reservations, I had to trust in His plan. I had to experience the burden of ministry and even learn how to serve when I didn't feel good. I learned how to be faithful to God and my leader no matter what. It was hard especially because I didn't feel worthy of the position but it was my assignment from God. I know I have been created to serve. Once I got over my emotions I began to believe that God was raising me up for reason. I begin to walk in it and work it! There were certainly days of being weary in well doing and times of dealing with people who honestly didn't care for me. Somehow, I had to learn how to still smile and keep going through it all. I had no ideas that everything that I was going through in ministry was just a blueprint to teach me how to run Regal Touch.

When I lost my job, one of the first things I thought to do was to serve full time in ministry. I serve in my church by giving of my time and talent and I wanted to help my pastor. In the beginning because business was still slow, I went up to the church daily to see what my pastor needed me to do. I would clean around the church without asking for a penny. As business increased it became a little hard but I knew that my faithfulness was what had caused my business to increase. I knew that what God was doing in my business was a result of my obedience to God and leadership. I'll never forgot what my grandfather in ministry told me. He said that God would bless my business if I stayed connected to my pastor. Who would've thought that Regal Touch was intertwined with my faithfulness to ministry.

As business grew, ministry grew to be more difficult. I was tired from working so much but running to get to church even if I was late. I was grateful that God was blessing me and causing business to grow rapidly like it was doing. I tried not to complain because it was a blessing. Many people don't survive in business a year or even six months! There were many days that I felt like staying home from church not because I didn't want to go but I was tired from working crazy hours. I would push myself to get up and go on Sunday mornings. Keep in mind, I still had to go in there with a smile on my face, knowing that people were watching me. I couldn't afford a bad day and I couldn't be off because they would talk.

So, I had to fake it until I was able to make it. I was a leader and as a leader there was no one else better to show the people how to have faith in the midst of adversity. Sometimes, I would go in there with no money in my pockets, truck on Empty, wondering how we would eat after church. I still would tithe and give what I was supposed to. I had crazy faith to believe God would do it for me and supply my needs. Trust me, He did! There was never a time where God did not come through for me and my family. We never went without anything. No I didn't have everything I wanted but I wasn't in need either. The more God showed His faithfulness to me, the more He sustained me. I continued to give and never thought twice about if I would make it. I had begun to see God move in my life and show forth His glory in my situations. I kept trusting even when it got hard.

I went through a season in church where it seemed like every week my pastor was ministering to my situation and encouraging me through the Word not to give up. One night after a week full of church and working doing the day, I remember asking God some more questions. Well, it was actually one specific questions that I had asked before. Can I really handle all of this? It's getting to be a bit much. I remember hearing Him say, "It's only the beginning. I've equipped you for it." Honestly, I wasn't trying to hear that but I knew God was my only source and reason for where I was.

I kept pressing and pushing through ministry and I often found myself wondering if things would ever get any easier. It seemed like my pastor wouldn't let up on me and he kept giving me more responsibilities. I would get so angry with him because it seemed to me that he didn't care about how tired I was. He kept pushing me to serve. I admit that I started to quit ministry! I just wanted to go to church and give my tithe and leave. My only off day was Sunday because I promised God when I started

Regal Touch that I wouldn't let nothing or no one get in the way of me being faithful to the One who got me going. Even so, I was tired and I didn't know if it was my fault that business was booming or God's!! I honestly wanted to blame God because He had told me that everything I touched He would bless and it was happening.

I know it sounds crazy but it seemed as if the more I pressed and praised, the more opportunities increased. It was to the point that I believed God was truly listening to my prayers but I still had a problem. How do I handle the prayers he was answering?

Couldn't nobody tell me that God wasn't faithful to His Word and promise to me. My issue was that I felt like I didn't have enough time to get it all done. I was always running late to church services, barely making meetings, drinking coffee to give me energy because I was sleepy. I still couldn't get it all together. I didn't have the manpower to hire someone to run my administration to give me a break. I was trying to fulfill my ministry duties and keep up with my business. How do I fit it all in and not break down? How do I still be effective and faithful all while smiling? How do I answer all my calls, pray with people, visit the sick, and make appointments for Regal Touch? Every time I wanted to tell my pastor that I couldn't do this anymore, I always forgot, or he was busy and I would change my mind. One day I said to him, "How do you do it all as a husband, father, pastor, and entrepreneur?" His reply was, "I give time to what matters most. My time is valuable so I only use it where I feel it's worth it."

In my mind, everywhere that I was spending my time was important. The problem was that I just didn't have enough time in the day to get everything done. At times, I became so engulfed in ministry that I forgot I still had kids at home who needed me first. Yes, building Regal Touch was how they ate and lived but they didn't ask for me to be gone from sunup and sundown. Yes, the money was a huge step up for my family from the money that I had made at the job I had for six years. The money was great but my relationship with my kids needed to improve. Yes, when it came to ministry they were at church with me involved in ministry as well but that still wasn't fair to them because they didn't get time with me personally. I didn't want them to start hating church and Regal Touch.

I knew how it was to grow up in the church and only know church. I was the only kid and church kids were my friends because I wasn't allowed to play with other people's kids! It seemed like my mom opened the doors of the church and she closed them. My life wasn't like regular kids. I played church but I didn't know how to jump double dutch. I practiced reading scriptures to my teddy bears but I couldn't skate. I preached my first sermon before a room full of stuffed animals but I couldn't swim. I was working media ministry at age ten while other kids were having sleepovers. I missed out on some things mainly because my mother couldn't afford to take me to fun places like other kids. Then when we had the money she had made other commitments.

I knew that girls deserved more than that. I wanted to give them vacations and spontaneous outings to do fun things without me having to worry how my bills would get paid when we got back home. It had been hard on them for many years because some of the things they wanted, I wasn't able to provide. Now, I was able to get those things but didn't have time to spend with them.

Now don't get me wrong. I'm truly grateful for what I saw and experienced because it made me who I am today. However, when I was going through those things ,it didn't feel good and I didn't enjoy it. I knew the girls were aware of what was going on and that were proud of me. Yet, I still knew that they deserved my time too. I already felt like ministry was starting to be too much for me and know the business was added to the mix as well. Nevertheless, the girls were my first and major priority. I needed to figure things out! I needed balance. Regal

Touch was starting to feel overwhelming, I needed more time with my kids, and I couldn't give up on God. Something had to give and the more I would try to make time ,the more customers would call. Honestly I was taking every client we could get because I didn't know the business time span for Regal.

I hated to miss any type of money because Regal still wasn't stable as a business. I knew that was the real cause behind me being tired and feeling overwhelmed. So I began to ask God for wisdom because I wanted to keep making money but I wanted to live to enjoy the fruit of my labor. God was expanding Regal Touch in such a way that I didn't want to miss the next wave of wind that He was blowing our way.

In the midst of all this, I started losing friends and those around me that I thought were genuinely for me. I was busy all of the time. I was building a business from the ground up and I figured that those closest to me would understand but that wasn't the case. The whispers behind my back and the talks about me continued. I was getting all types of questions like, Are you still working the cleaning business? Did you get another job yet? How you making it? It was becoming increasingly annoying and a slap in my face that people was really saying I couldn't make it in my business.

The hatred was real but it fueled my fire to push myself and Regal Touch further to succeed. I begin see people differently and I stopped letting people's opinions and comments affect my progress. It was time to walk alone and leave the critics behind. My skin had to grow a little thicker. I got to a place where I believed in myself and that was all that mattered. It amazed me that once my mind was made up, things began to fall into place. I was no longer waiting for the approval of others for my business. This was what the Lord had placed in my hands to do and I was going to get it accomplished no matter what. Yes, there were plenty days of loneliness and missing out on things that I wanted to attend but I knew that building my brand was more important. I felt like real friends would understand and not make me feel bad for missing out on things.

Then I also knew that real friends where concerned about me learning how to juggle it all and have fun! I knew eventually I couldn't just work and never enjoy life. I just needed time to build a firm foundation before going out and having fun.

One thing I had learned, was that anybody can make money but very few people know how to keep it! Honestly, that was my goal to make money for the generation after me. I observed how so many nationalities create wealth for their grandchildren before they are born. I felt like if I was going to work hard I wanted to make sure I leave seed in the ground so my great grandchildren can reap a harvest! So if I got to lose friends on the way up it's worth it!

My relationship with my daughters and my friends weren't the only relationships in trouble. My love life was in the pits! It was already difficult dating as a female minister but now being a business owner added more stress to it. I was the owner of Regal Touch but I also worked like everyone else. There were many times that I had to cancel dates because of work related issues. Then the only time that I had available to date was late in the evenings when I got off. That wasn't a good look for me to be out dating late at night but I never had time before 9:00 PM to do anything. As I stated, Sundays were dedicated to church during the day and during the evening and at night I would try and catch up on my rest as much as possible. I felt bad because I wanted God to bless me with someone but I didn't have the time to set aside to date him properly or show interest. *What do I do?* I didn't have an answer so I continued to work. Skip a man!

I started putting up a wall by telling myself that everything was okay and that I was making money and my girls and I would be fine. *I don't need a man!* Well, I was feeling this way because I didn't know how to make time. I was already feeling the pressure of managing so much that I just didn't want the pressure of a man saying that I didn't have time for him. I figured that as long as I went out with my friends I would be be okay. Maybe God had already given me everything that I needed.

One day the Lord reminded me again that He would give me the things that I asked for but I had to be honest. By psyching myself up saying that I didn't need or want a man was not helping me. Me saying that I didn't have time for a relationship wasn't helping me. I was learning that what I was speaking out my mouth was manifesting and if I wasn't careful of what I spoke I could cause a curse upon myself. I begin to stop placing what I thought was too much on me and started placing it on God. I begin to look at successful business people with healthy marriages, family life, and profitable businesses. It wasn't so much that I needed a relationship in this moment of my career but it was more about taking the limitations off of God. I trusted Him with Regal Touch so why couldn't He take care of the other areas of my life? Truthfully, I wanted someone rooting, cheering, and pushing for me.

It seems like if it wasn't one thing it was another! After a while, I found myself stressing out. My eating habits were all over the place because I would eat while I was on the move. I wasn't exercising because I was so tired all of the time. I would work all day then get home too late to eat properly. I was trying to juggle it all and there were many days It where I didn't know if I was coming or going. I was misplacing things and getting to the point that I started feeling like I was losing my mind. At first I was just excusing everything as being a part of trying to get a handle on balancing business ownership and everyday life. Then I realized that wasn't the issue.

The stress came from having to solely depend on myself to make decisions regarding my business. Yes, God was leading me but at the end of the day, I had to put in the work. I had a lot of responsibility. I finally had started hiring people. That meant that people were depending on me to pay them. There were days that I felt like a heavy weight was on my shoulders. I didn't want my decisions to hurt myself or anyone that was associated with my business. Sometimes the pressure of it all kept me up tossing and turning at night. Yes, money was coming in but it was also going right out of the door. I wasn't seeing real profit, which I learned that most business owners wouldn't see for at least the first three years of being in business. Even when people told me that business tidbit, I didn't receive it. I learned early on in business that what you speak over your business can cause it to manifest. Even when going through I always made sure I spoke life over my business. So even through the stressful moments I still had sense to watch what I said concerning Regal Touch.

I knew that having good health was linked to my business as well. I knew that if I wanted to see real success and enjoy the fruit of my labor, I had to be concerned about my health. My body had a way of knocking me down when I didn't get enough rest. I remember that one day while I was driving I began to get light headed. I knew it was because I had not been getting enough rest. My health was failing me slowly but surely. Headaches and body aches were becoming way too common. I started trying to hide my weakness and pain by taking pain pills, pushing along, and praying. Sadly, I still hadn't taken enough measures to improve my health. Things began to get so bad that there were times that I started sneaking to the emergency room in the middle of the night.

I made sure that I would go after work while the kids were sleep. When I got released, I would come home, get up and go to work or to church, and even take the girls to school given the day, like nothing was wrong.

Sadly, I had become good at putting on a facade. This strong faced woman was never able to show any signs of weakness. I had to have it all together at all times. But the truth was that I was falling apart. I was trying to manage everything but it had got to point that my body was overpowering my mind. I couldn't give up because I knew Regal Touch was destined for greatness. I just needed to manage my life in a way that I could be healthy and as stress free as possible. The fact of the matter was that life was going to keep moving with or without me figuring out how to do it all. I just had to learn how to breathe through it all.

It was time to work smart and not hard! Word of mouth became my new marketing manager and it was working. Calls and emails were coming in without posting and fishing for work. The calendar was filling up with work and it felt good!. Even though I had moments of missing out on fun, dating, and friends, it was worth it to see hard work paying off in such a short time. Things I had been praying for concerning the business were coming to past. I couldn't stop now because I knew my journey was a blueprint for someone else to follow. I purposely adjusted my outlook and my mindset and as a result I began to view my experience as a bridge to carry others into better opportunities.

I couldn't let the moments of weakness stop me. What had started as a means for me to support my own family had grown into a business that helped to provide income to support other families. I had started with nothing. Somehow, I had preserved to earn more money in my first year as a business owner than I had earned at working for others at previous jobs. I had stopped working and struggling paycheck to paycheck. I was no longer borrowing money and putting myself in deeper debt or pushing someone else's vision while my dreams were just ideas. I had found my niche and I was determined to keep climbing the ladder of success. I had successfully made it from buckets to big bucks.

I had redeveloped my focus. Sure, I still had things to learn and changes to make but with God I was well on my way to unimagined success.

9

EPILOGUE

I look back at a situation that was meant to break me. It was designed to make me start over and give up. Being a single mom in her late thirties with no formal education to fall back on was destined to break me. Ultimately, I found myself and my destiny in a cleaning bucket. Who would've thought that a bucket of cleaning supplies would turn into big bucks?

I can't say that "I have arrived" but I can say that I am well on my way. If nothing, I have learned that it's not about how you start a thing but the road you take to continue it. I wasn't sure where the road was taking me when I started this journey but I have learned to trust the process. Even on the bad days I found strength to continue on and the good days were just a bonus to remind me not to quit because Regal Touch will be great one day.

I was warned that Regal Touch would take a lot of work, time, and money to succeed. Many told me to give up and go back to a regular job. I can truthfully say that those people were 100% correct. It does takes a lot of time to see every idea through to completion. It takes money to grow your business and work is all you do until things get better.

In hindsight, I could have gone back to my comfort zone of working in fast food restaurant management which is something that I had done most of my life. I could have gotten a regular job doing anything just to support my family. However, my destiny was interrupted by desperation. I couldn't take a job just to be doing something. I had to do what I was destined to do. What would have happen if I didn't get fired? Would I have stayed wanting and wishing for a better life for my family while pushing someone else's dream forward? Sadly, in most cases that's usually how it works. You sit around pushing someone else's dreams and visions all while wanting a better life for yourself but never doing anything to change the situation. When is enough enough? How do you go from having barely enough to living in abundance?

I was always one who had dreams and aspirations but life hit hard for me at an early age so I gave up and went into survival mode. Survival mode is dangerous because people tend to get comfortable in existing without producing anything. In survival mode you often see life through a looking glass and it looks like there isn't a way out. It seems like those around you are prospering, getting married, obtaining degrees, and traveling the country. Personally, it wasn't until my glass was shattered into pieces that I realized that the opportunity for freedom existed once more again. Truthfully, at times it takes shattered glass to bring your life into full circle. I found out that the greatness inside of me had not changed. It had just been dormant and was hiding under the rocks and boulders of life. Well, Regal Touch was a major awakening in my life and it has made me want to reach out and encourage others to know that it is never too late to go after your dreams.

What took me one year to accomplish took others three to seven years to perform. Business has taken off like a jet without a landing strip in sight. In fact, I couldn't even celebrate the one year anniversary like I planned because Regal Touch was super busy during that time. Towards the last quarter, things really did change. Contracts started coming in. Contracts were something that I had prayed for because I desired more consistent money to support the business. In fact, business finances changed to the point that I was filing taxes for Regal Touch and for myself as well. Who would've thought that would be my story? I went from waiting on my tax return to now filing taxes and hoping that I didn't owe anything. Things had really begun to grow in ways that I couldn't imagine. Days of sitting on the internet posting Regal Touch fliers to gain business turned into needing a marketing specialist to help keep the brand going.

What do you do with unexpected growth? Growth is what every new business owner hopes for including myself but I wasn't prepared as I should of been. As I have grown, I've learned the importance of planning and setting goals. In fact, I have expanded my goals by creating a five year business plan. Yep, me the person that started with no plan at all is now working on five year plans. It just goes to show the maturity and growth that takes place in business and life and general.

I consistently review my goals for my business and from reading this book thus far you know that I'm all about asking questions and doing self-reflection. One of my main questions right now is, "Can I set Regal Touch up in such a way that it's attractive to buyers and investors?" You have to think about the future and not let the present hold you down.

Truthfully, financially speaking, because Regal is still a fairly new business there are a bit more liabilities than assets right now. However, I am actively working to get that together so that Regal continues to operate sufficiently with little to no debt. One of the biggest things I have learned is the importance of establishing business credit and separating my name from Regal Touch. It was a recurring issue even in year two but I refused to cry and complain about what I didn't have and what wasn't given to me. I have learned that every "No" is not personal. It's just "No" because you don't meet the qualifications that were set.

With changing my mindset, I have decided to start the road of recovery for my future. I am determined to not let Regal Touch fall through the cracks and I blame it on society. It's not society's fault that my credit was jacked up and that I wasn't able to obtain what I needed for Regal Touch. Playing the victim will not advance your business but having your business in order will.

Another key to my success came about because I changed my prices. I mentioned this a little earlier in the book but honestly I was extremely hesitant to change prices.

My business was centered around being a great cleaning service with a cheap price tag attached. Ultimately, I decided that instead of adjusting prices for different states, I would just go up on my prices across the board. I wasn't sure how the clients I already had would take it, so I kept them where they were in good faith hoping that because they were regular clients they wouldn't go anywhere. As customers would call and book appointments going forward, I started quoting the new prices and to my surprise everyone was still ok with it. It showed me that I would have hindered Regal Touch financially because I didn't fully believe in our business like I thought I did.

As I said before, you must believe in your own service or product more than anyone else! I wasn't raising prices to hurt my clientele but I raised prices because it was the best decision for Regal Touch. Price changes needed to happen because I was buying more supplies, hiring more employees, and my biggest goal was to see a profit in sales by the end of year two. Until my credit was repaired I still needed money prepared for hard times.

My hardest lesson overall may have been learning how to maintain clients. This was a difficult concept to learn because people will try you one time, pay you, send you on your way and never use you again. Depending on the service they receive they will tell someone if their experience was good or bad. At first, I was excited about getting more clients because that was an opportunity for more money. Well, I was excited until I realized that Regal Touch was receiving more new clients in a year than recurring ones. Now granted some people would hear this and have the conclusion that at least the business was making money.

However, I discovered that new clients are nice but new money has no loyalty to you like consistent money. With this thought in mind, I had to learn the difference between clients and customers. Clients have a budget they set aside and they figure you into that budget because they need your service. On the contrary, customers come and go. They call whenever they are in need. Now, don't get the wrong ideas because there is nothing wrong with that but in terms of a business standpoint you can't necessarily count on their money. I had a lot of customers in the first year. I couldn't complain about it because I needed the money and experience. Now a year later, we had found our worth and value it and that has made it easier to gage the clientele.

As a result, I stopped getting depressed about the revolving door of new customers and I focused my attention on ways to keep the loyal ones.

Another thing to note is the increase in commercial sales that Regal Touch has had. Regal is now servicing city buildings, real estate properties, banquet halls, condo buildings, office spaces, apartment co-ops, and industrial office sites. We started out with churches, barber shops, and beauty salons and look at us now. More work meant an increase in employees. In fact, what was three employees has now grown to be eleven employees. Additionally, Regal Touch has continued marketing on even more social media outlets. People are hearing more about the company and we are seeing more referrals.

Entrepreneurship hasn't been an easy journey but I have learned so much in a short period of time. Do I know all the answers to the questions? Absolutely not! However, I do know how to help you stay the course and not give up. It is my desire to use my experience gained on this journey to financial wealth and freedom and empower others along the way. I tell my story to offer hope to anyone with dreams of entrepreneurship. No matter what your current situation maybe it is never too late to go after your dreams.

www.ingramcontent.com/pod-product-compliance
Lightning Source LLC
Chambersburg PA
CBHW071416220526
45469CB00004B/1295